SY 0125816 8

KU-108-040

Developing Post-Primary Education in Sub-Saharan Africa

ASSESSING THE FINANCIAL SUSTAINABILITY OF ALTERNATIVE PATHWAYS

AFRICA HUMAN
DEVELOPMENT SERIES

Developing Post-Primary Education in Sub-Saharan Africa

ASSESSING THE FINANCIAL SUSTAINABILITY OF ALTERNATIVE PATHWAYS

AFRICA HUMAN
DEVELOPMENT SERIES

Alain Mingat, Blandine Ledoux,
and Ramahatra Rakotomalala

Note: The analysis and conclusions presented in this document are those of the authors alone.
They do not necessarily reflect the official position of the AFD or its partner institutions or that of the
World Bank, its affiliated organizations, and the members of its Board of Executive Directors and the
countries they represent. Any errors are the sole responsibility of the authors.

THE WORLD BANK
Washington, DC

© 2010 The International Bank for Reconstruction and Development / The World Bank
1818 H Street NW
Washington DC 20433
Telephone: 202-473-1000
Internet: www.worldbank.org
E-mail: feedback@worldbank.org

All rights reserved
1 2 3 4 13 12 11 10

This volume is a product of the staff of the International Bank for Reconstruction and Development / The World Bank. The findings, interpretations, and conclusions expressed in this volume do not necessarily reflect the views of the Executive Directors of The World Bank or the governments they represent.

The World Bank does not guarantee the accuracy of the data included in this work. The boundaries, colors, denominations, and other information shown on any map in this work do not imply any judgement on the part of The World Bank concerning the legal status of any territory or the endorsement or acceptance of such boundaries.

Rights and Permissions
The material in this publication is copyrighted. Copying and/or transmitting portions or all of this work without permission may be a violation of applicable law. The International Bank for Reconstruction and Development / The World Bank encourages dissemination of its work and will normally grant permission to reproduce portions of the work promptly.

For permission to photocopy or reprint any part of this work, please send a request with complete information to the Copyright Clearance Center Inc., 222 Rosewood Drive, Danvers, MA 01923, USA; telephone: 978-750-8400; fax: 978-750-4470; Internet: www.copyright.com.

All other queries on rights and licenses, including subsidiary rights, should be addressed to the Office of the Publisher, The World Bank, 1818 H Street NW, Washington, DC 20433, USA; fax: 202-522-2422; e-mail: pubrights@worldbank.org.

ISBN: 978-0-8213-8183-0
eISBN: 978-0-8213-8236-3
DOI: 10.1596/978-0-8213-8183-0

Cover photo: Ramahatra Rakotomalala

Library of Congress Cataloging-in-Publication Data
Developing post-primary education in Sub-Saharan Africa: assessing the financial sustainability of alternative pathways.
    p. cm.
    Includes bibliographical references.
    1. Education, Secondary—Economic aspects—Africa, Sub-Saharan. 2. Education, Secondary—Africa, Sub-Saharan—Finance. 3. Sustainable development—Africa, Sub-Saharan.
    LC67.58.A357D48 2010
    373.67—dc22
                                                                    2009052116

Table of Contents

Foreword

Many African countries are eager to sharpen their competitive edge in today's global economy. Attaining long-term sustainable growth through a diversified and competitive economy, improving governance, empowering people, and mitigating environmental risks are some of the crucial challenges they face in the coming years. Because these challenges cannot be met without qualified human resources, investments in education must deliver quality basic education for all and produce the skilled professionals required to support economic growth strategies.

Most African countries have achieved remarkable progress toward universal primary school completion over the last decade, averaging a 15 percentage-point gain between 2000 and 2007. In the coming years, primary school enrollments are expected to continue expanding as domestic and international efforts to advance the Education Millennium Development Goals (MDGs) bear fruit. Success on this front will make a major contribution to Africa's renaissance and economic competitiveness.

The surge in primary school completion has had a knock-on impact on secondary (general and vocational) and tertiary education. The social demand for post-primary education is growing rapidly as increasing numbers of primary school leavers seek to continue their schooling. There are signs, however, that the trend is putting significant pressure on the education system, often straining its capacity to deliver services that meet minimal quality standards. In some countries, unemployment among educated youth is an increasing concern, given the still-limited absorptive capacity of the labor market. These emerging problems raise questions about the social and financial sustainability of current policies and motivate the need for thoughtful reflection on the trade-offs that may be required to reconcile competing priorities amidst constrained resources.

African countries differ widely in terms of pattern of enrollments, unit costs, student flow management, and resource mobilization. The intensity and nature of the challenges they face are therefore quite diverse, which means that policies must be tailored to each country's particular circumstances. Nonetheless, a comparative analysis of post-primary education across the 33 Sub-Saharan African (SSA) low-income countries with added reference to other regions and also to middle-income countries, can offer a useful lens for assessing needs and constraints and for drawing lessons from the diversity of education across countries.

To provide this comparative lens, the Agence Française de Développement (AFD) and the World Bank (WB) embarked on a joint analytical effort. A research team was set up in 2007, comprising Professor Alain Mingat from the University of Bourgogne, Blandine Ledoux (AFD), and Ramahatra Rakotomalala (WB), to prepare the analysis under the direction of Jean-Claude Balmes (AFD) and Jee-Peng Tan (WB), with assistance from Kirsten Majgaard (WB). Their effort builds on the earlier work that helped define the Fast Track Initiative (FTI) indicative framework for primary education and has produced a new tool that is both more comprehensive, covering all levels of the system, and more sensitive to the conditions in low-income countries. The findings of the study were first presented at the 2008 Biennale of the Association for the Development of Education in Africa (ADEA) in Maputo. Subsequently, the results were shared with members of the Catalytic Fund Committee of the Education for All Fast Track Initiative (EFA-FTI) at their September 2008 meeting in Paris, and also with participants at the July 2009 Conference for African Ministers of Finance and of Education that was organized by the World Bank, the African Development Bank, and ADEA.

Among the study's most compelling findings is the scale of the pressure on the education system in most African countries. If current trends persist in the next decade, enrollments at the primary and secondary levels are projected to multiply by a factor between 1.8 and 14. The cost of service delivery in secondary and tertiary education, as reflected in public spending per student, is on average three times as high in Africa as in other regions of the world. While there is great variability across countries, a consideration of the projected size of the enrollments and cost patterns leads to the stark conclusion that a laissez-faire approach is likely to produce a downward spiral of continuous deterioration in education quality.

Given the diversity across African countries, this study offers no generic policy fix. Rather, it is intended as an analytical tool for national leaders and their development partners to inform discussion and debate about alternative options in light of country circumstances. The simulation scenarios it presents therefore serve an illustrative function, to draw attention to options such as raising the share of education in the national budget, reforming the service delivery arrangements to manage costs, diversifying the student flow beyond lower secondary education, enlarging the role of private funding, particularly in post-primary education, and so on. Helpfully, the study captures the nature of the choices by presenting alternative packages of policies, using them to clarify the affordability of what the authors characterize as "spartan" and "generous" choices. The simulation model's flexibility can be exploited to adapt the package of policies to suit national contexts. This feature is perhaps one of the study's most valuable contributions.

We hope that this joint work sponsored by our respective organizations will prove useful to all—governments, experts and funding agencies alike—and that it will contribute to the design of holistic and sustainable education policies to help advance educational development in Africa in the coming years.

Michel Jacquier   Yaw Ansu
Deputy CEO   Director of Human Development
AFD   Africa Region, World Bank

Acknowledgments

This study was prepared by a joint team from the Agence Française de Développement and the World Bank that includes Alain Mingat (IREDU–CNRS and the University of Bourgogne), Blandine Ledoux (AFD), and Ramahatra Rakotomalala (WB). Kirsten Majgaard (WB) assisted the team in finalizing the report.

The authors thank the country teams from the six Sub-Saharan African countries (Republic of Congo, Ghana, Guinea, Niger, Sierra Leone, and Tanzania) who participated in two multicountry workshops conducted in early 2008 to test and adapt the simulation model. The workshops improved the simulation model in several important ways.

Many other individuals contributed to the study. Jean-Claude Balmes (AFD), Jee-Peng Tan (WB), and Yaw Ansu (WB) provided overall leadership and guidance. Further, the study benefited from constructive feedback from Sajitha Bashir, Jacob Bregman, Barbara Bruns, Paul Coustere, William Experton, Birger Fredriksen, Jean-Pierre Jarousse, Thomas Melonio, Aidan Mulkeen, Steven Obeegadoo, Bob Prouty, Michel Welmond, and many others. Marjorie Leach translated the draft report.

The authors also acknowledge the generous financial support of the Agence Française de Développement and the Norwegian Post-Primary Education Fund.

Abbreviations

AFD	Agence Française de Développement
ADEA	Association for the Development of Education in Africa
BREDA	UNESCO Regional Office for Education
EdStats	World Bank Education Statistics
EFA	Education for All
Enrollm.	enrollment
ES	enrollment scenario
FTI	Fast Track Initiative
GDP	gross domestic product
GER	gross enrollment ratio
GNI	gross national income
IBRD	International Bank for Reconstruction and Development
IDA	International Development Association
IMF	International Monetary Fund
MDG	Millennium Development Goal
P	primary
S1	lower secondary
S2	upper secondary
SSA	Sub-Saharan Africa—usually used to indicate the 33 SSA countries in the study
TVET	technical and vocational education and training
UIS	UNESCO Institute for Statistics
UN	United Nations
UNESCO	United Nations Educational, Scientific, and Cultural Organization

Note: All dollar amounts are U.S. dollars (US$) unless otherwise indicated.

Executive Summary

RECENT ACCOMPLISHMENTS AND PROSPECTS FOR GROWTH IN COVERAGE AND ENROLLMENTS

Primary school completion rates in Sub-Saharan Africa (SSA) have been rising rapidly in recent years. Across the 33 low-income SSA countries that are the focus of this study, they have climbed from an average of 43 percent in 1999 to 53 percent in 2005, a rate that exceeds the increase of the 1990s. As a result of this salutary trend, the absolute number of primary school completers has been rising steadily and will continue to do so as SSA countries press on toward the goal of universal primary school completion. For example, if all SSA countries attained a primary completion rate of 95 percent by 2020, the 33 SSA countries would have a total of 22.2 million primary school completers in 2020, compared with 9.4 million around 2005, an increase of a factor of 2.4 over the period.

In most SSA countries, the projected increase will inevitably put pressure on all levels of the education system, but particularly at the secondary and tertiary levels. The intensity of the pressure is likely to vary from country to country, depending on factors such as demography, the speed of progress toward universal primary completion, and changes in transition rates between various cycles of education. For example, if the transition rate between primary and lower secondary education rises to 100 percent, projected enrollments in lower secondary education in 2020 as a multiple of enrollments around the mid-2000s would be around 2 times in Lesotho, Togo, and Zimbabwe; close to 4 times in Guinea and Mali; around 9 times in Burundi, Tanzania, and Uganda; and more than 11 times in Mozambique and Niger.

SIMULATION MODEL TO ASSESS POLICY OPTIONS

Given the scale of the projected enrollment increases, countries in SSA should find it timely to take stock of the implications for policy development. A key challenge is to ensure that the education system continues to develop in an efficient, equitable, and fiscally sustainable manner, even as it expands to accommodate the rising numbers seeking a place in secondary and tertiary education.

Policy makers therefore face a difficult task: They must grapple with the inherent tensions between choosing outcomes that are desirable (for example, meeting the educational aspirations of all youths and responding to employers' needs for skilled labor) and those that are feasible in a given time frame and financially sustainable over the medium term. They also confront choices that must achieve a sustainable balance between national goals for economic and social development and the social demands of individuals—two impulses that often pull in opposite directions. Furthermore, in choosing among the alternatives, policy makers will quickly realize that actions taken at one level of education cannot be isolated from those taken either upstream or downstream. Each subsector is part of the same systemic architecture and depends on the same overall resource envelope, whether funded by domestic or foreign sources. A holistic approach is thus highly desirable and indeed unavoidable.

To help clarify the policy options, this study constructed a sectorwide education simulation model to simulate the financial implications of alternative policy choices. Although the model pays specific attention to post-primary education and training (which here comprises lower and upper secondary education, technical and vocational training, and higher education), it incorporates policies in all the subsectors simultaneously in the simulations. The results thus provide a basis for assessing alternative options not only in each subsystem but also for the system as a whole. The results are an aggregation of simulations specific to each of the 33 low-income SSA countries in the study. The findings provide a rich basis for policy dialogue within each country and between the countries and their development partners.

The simulation model is designed to address fundamental questions such as (1) How much domestic resources can countries themselves reasonably mobilize for education? (2) How much foreign aid can the donor nations realistically contribute to the sector? (3) What are acceptable levels of dependency on external aid in recipient and donor countries alike? and (4) What reforms in education sector policies—in terms of the pattern of coverage by level and type of education and of service delivery arrangements—will be required to put the education system on a sustainable path? In today's climate of global economic slowdown, such analysis has become especially pertinent.

Three sets of policy parameters give the model its basic structure: enrollments, cost drivers, and financing arrangements. To illustrate the implications of alternative choices, the study focused on a few specific options within these parameters. While the simulation tool can be used to explore additional scenarios pertinent to country-specific circumstances, the generic scenarios presented below already provide a useful overview of the challenges that most SSA countries are likely to face in finding a sustainable approach for developing post-primary education.

OPTIONS PERTAINING TO ENROLLMENT

The simulations explored five enrollment scenarios (ES), the first two of which are distinctly different from the next three in terms of student flow management. In particular, the first two scenarios (ES-1 and ES-2) envision progress toward universal or nearly universal primary completion by 2020 and wide coverage in the lower secondary cycle, followed by transition into tertiary education at current rates of transition from the previous cycle. In addition, the scenarios envision some diversification of educational options in the form of school-to-work life skills training and formal technical and vocational education and training. The other set of three enrollment scenarios (ES-3, ES-4, and ES-5) envision similar goals for coverage in primary and lower secondary education as in ES-1 and ES-2, but explicitly calibrates enrollments in tertiary education (and hence of upper secondary education) to expected employment opportunities in the formal sector of the economy. Because this sector is expected to remain relatively small in the foreseeable future, coverage at the upper levels of the system is expected to remain limited. At the same time, the scenarios envision greater provision of school-to-work transition options intended to relieve the pressure on the formal education system, particularly at the upper secondary and tertiary levels. The last simulation scenario, ES-5, corresponds to the option of combining the primary and lower secondary cycle into a basic education cycle. This option is of interest mainly because it reflects an organizational strategy to manage the cost of service delivery.

OPTIONS PERTAINING TO COST DRIVERS

The second set of options relates to policies on service delivery that affect the cost of services. In primary education, these factors include variables such as the pupil-teacher ratio, average teacher salaries, and spending on non-teacher inputs. This study uses the same values for these parameters as the FTI benchmarks, except for the poorest countries, where the value for teacher salaries is adjusted for a country's income level. In secondary education, two sets of parameter values are used in the simulations, one to mirror relatively "generous" (that is, more expensive) service delivery arrangements in terms of class size, teacher salaries, teaching loads, instructional time, and spending on non-teacher inputs, and the other to mirror relatively "spartan" (that is, more economical) arrangements. The parameters relating to life skills training, technical and vocational education and training (TVET), and tertiary education are specified directly in terms of spending per student, and the values for these parameters are linked proportionally to the level of spending per student in secondary school. In addition, for tertiary education, the model differentiates spending per student by field of study and computes overall average spending per student by weighting the field-specific spending by the corresponding distribution of enrollment by field of study.

The simulation model also includes parameters for capital costs for the construction of additional classrooms in primary and secondary schools to accommodate growing student enrollments in these cycles. The model computes capital costs simply as a function of the choice of enrollment scenario (ES-1 to ES-5), the class size, and a standard unit construction cost applied to all the 33 countries. Capital costs for tertiary education and TVET are excluded for lack of a reasonable basis for establishing benchmarks that might apply to the whole sample of countries in the study.

OPTIONS PERTAINING TO PUBLIC AND PRIVATE RESOURCES FOR EDUCATION

The third set of assumptions relates to resource mobilization, both in terms of government allocation of public budgets and the distribution between publicly funded and privately funded enrollments. For resource mobilization, the parameter values are the same as those in the Education for All–Fast Track Initiative (EFA-FTI) framework, while those for the public-private shares are chosen to reflect policy choices that take into account concerns about equity and efficiency. Thus, the values for the share of privately funded services are set at a modest level of about 10 percent for primary and lower secondary education and related school-to-work transition programs, but at a much higher rate of about 40 percent for courses of study beyond lower secondary education. These figures take into consideration the high social impact of primary and lower secondary education, which justifies public spending, as well as the high private rate of return of tertiary education, which would imply a greater scope for private funding.

USING MORE FLEXIBLE PARAMETER VALUES FOR THE SIMULATIONS

In the indicative framework of the EFA-FTI, only one set of benchmarks is used regardless of country context. While this standard approach can facilitate an analysis involving a large number of countries, it tends to reduce the persuasiveness of the results for particular countries. The FTI benchmark of 3.5 times the per capita gross domestic product (GDP) for teacher salaries, for example, has been singled out as being particularly inappropriate in the poorest countries. Where the per capita GDP is $100 or less, for example, the benchmark implies a level of pay that often falls below the poverty line. In the present study, important features have been incorporated to overcome these flaws, including linking to the per capita GDP the assumed parameter values for teacher salary and also adjusting for the distribution of the population between urban and rural areas. The latter variable affects costs to the extent that services are more costly to deliver in rural than urban settings, as well as to the extent that demand-side interventions may be required in rural areas to enroll the remaining pockets of children who have not attended school.

SIMULATION RESULTS

The simulations demonstrate that funding gaps are highly sensitive to the choice of policies in all three areas captured by the model, that is, coverage or enrollment, service delivery, and financing arrangements.

In a scenario that combines the most expansive policy for coverage (ES-1), the more input-intensive of two possible assumptions for service delivery, and a 20 percent share of education in overall government spending (and assuming a real GDP per capita growth of 2 percent per year), the resulting aggregate gap in recurrent funding in 2020 for the 33 countries would amount to $29.1 billion a year for post-primary education and $3.1 billion a year for primary education (for a systemwide total of $32.2 billion a year). In addition, these countries would have a funding gap for capital investments in primary and secondary education of about $2.8 billion a year. Filling the gaps with external funds would imply that 68 percent of total aggregate expenditures would rely on outside sources, which is a very high rate of dependency, possibly an unrealistic one. With slightly less ambitious goals for coverage (that is, a transition rate between primary and lower secondary education of 80 percent instead of 100 percent), as captured by scenario ES-2, the gap in recurrent expenditure in 2020 would be $22.7 billion a year for post-primary education and $3.1 billion for primary education (for a systemwide total of $25.8 billion a year), and the gap in capital spending on primary and secondary education would be $2.5 billion a year. Correspondingly, the level of aid dependency would fall only slightly, to 63 percent, which is clearly not fundamentally distinct from the first scenario in terms of the fiscal sustainability of the policies.

The next three enrollment scenarios, ES-3 to ES-5, mark a clear-cut departure from the previous two in that they reflect much more selective policies for coverage in upper secondary and tertiary education. However, even in the most restrictive of these scenarios, ES-5, the recurrent funding gap is projected at $3.4 billion a year for post-basic education and $5.2 billion a year for basic education, (a 9-year cycle in ES-5. This gives a systemwide total of $8.6 billion a year), while the gap in capital funding for basic and secondary education is projected at $2.6 billion a year. The dependency ratio would be 40 percent if the policies for service delivery were to favor the more input-intensive options and the share of education in total government spending were limited to 20 percent. With more economical options for service delivery, an increase in the share of government financing to at least 23 percent, and restrained expansion of upper secondary and tertiary education, the systemwide recurrent funding gap could be brought down to $6.5 billion a year and the dependency ratio would then fall below 35 percent.

CONCLUSIONS

This study finds that, in all the policy scenarios considered, the development of post-primary education in the 33 SSA countries would require sizable amounts of external aid to fill funding gaps. If a dependency rate of 35 percent represents a sort of upper bound that most SSA countries and their donor partners prefer not to exceed, some clear conclusions can be distilled from the simulation results. First, policies that envision massification of the first cycle of secondary education combined with continuity of student flow at subsequent levels would generally be untenable. Staying within the 35 percent threshold will typically require policies that regulate student flow more actively. Second, between the generous and spartan options for service delivery, the latter will probably be the choice that would allow most SSA countries to expand post-primary education without exceeding the 35 percent threshold for dependency on external funding. Third, for most SSA countries, an allocation of 23 percent of total public spending for the education sector may be required to avoid an untenable dependency on external aid to finance educational development. Competing needs from other sectors may make it difficult to attain this level of spending everywhere, but a share lower than 20 percent would in most of the sample countries jeopardizes achievement of universal basic education along with a reasonable pace of development in post-basic education.

While the broad conclusions drawn from the simulations point to the common challenges faced by the 33 SSA countries included in this study, the degree of their relevance will depend on each country's initial conditions and political context. Given the diversity in the pressures on enrollment, the cost of service delivery, and the potential for resource mobilization, policies will clearly need to be tailored accordingly. For this reason, the results reported in this study are merely indicative and must be complemented by additional country-specific analysis. Such analysis can be prepared using the tool developed for this study or other similar models that permit an assessment using a sectorwide framework in which key policy choices in the main subsectors of the education system are given explicit consideration.

CHAPTER 1

Introduction

A ll countries in Sub-Saharan Africa (SSA) face the prospect of a substantial increase in the number of primary school completers in the coming years. Although initial conditions vary widely from country to country, this increase will inevitably intensify pressure on the education system, particularly at the secondary and tertiary levels. African countries may thus find it timely to align their education policies and strategies to the emerging challenges. A key goal is to ensure that the education system continues to develop in an efficient, equitable, and fiscally sustainable manner even as it expands to accommodate the rising numbers seeking a place in secondary and tertiary education.

In evaluating the policy options, decision makers cannot easily ignore the inherent tensions involved, particularly between outcomes that are desirable (such as meeting the educational aspirations of all youths and responding to employers' needs for skilled labor) and those that are feasible in a given time frame and financially sustainable over the medium term. Decision makers must also balance national goals for economic and social development with the social demands of individuals—two impulses that often pull in opposite directions. Furthermore, in choosing among the alternatives, policy makers will quickly realize that actions taken at one level of education cannot be isolated from those taken either upstream or downstream. A holistic approach is required simply because each subsector is part of the same systemic architecture and depends on the same overall resource envelope, whether funded by domestic or foreign sources (see, for example, Hoppers and Obeegadoo 2008).

Policy makers thus face a difficult task. This study seeks to clarify the options available to them, focusing in particular on post-primary education and training, which is defined here as comprising the two subcycles of secondary education, technical and vocational training and higher education. It examines policy options in each of these subsystems as well as the package of choices taken as a whole. The results rely on a simulation model and are based on data for 33 low-income[1] SSA countries.[2]

The rest of this report is organized as follows. Chapter 2 elaborates the policy context for education development in SSA. Chapter 3 explains the methodology and data sources. Chapter 4 examines the challenges and constraints posed by the sheer volume of increases in enrollments in post-primary education with which most education systems in SSA must grapple in the coming years. Taking these constraints into account, the report evaluates the scope for policy development from three perspectives in the subsequent chapters: the coverage of education systems (chapter 5), the quality and cost of service delivery (chapter 6), and the division of financing by public and private sources (chapter 7). The fiscal implications of plausible policy packages that SSA countries might consider[3] are assessed in chapter 8. Chapter 9 seems up the general conclusions of the report.

NOTES

1. Low-income countries are here defined as countries eligible for lending from the International Development Association (IDA). These countries had a 2006 gross national income (GNI) per capita income of less than $1,065 per year. The threshold changes every year as do the countries' per capita incomes, so there may be small changes from year to year in this group.

2. This group of countries is the same as that used in Bruns, Mingat, and Rakotomalala (2003), the study that estimated the cost and financing gaps to universalize primary school completion by 2015 and provided the analytical foundations for the indicative framework of the EFA-FTI launched in 2002.

3. This study complements that of Lewin (2008), and the overall conclusions of the two studies are consistent.

CHAPTER 2

The Policy Context

Africa n countries can take pride today in their unmistakable progress toward the Education for All (EFA) goals for 2015 that were agreed upon at the Dakar 2000 World Education Forum. The Dakar Forum galvanized action leading to increases in domestic and external funding for education in developing countries, particularly in Sub-Saharan Africa (SSA) and to the creation of a new partnership arrangement with donors, the EFA Fast Track Initiative (EFA-FTI), to help accelerate progress toward universal primary education. Economic conditions in most SSA countries have also been improving rapidly as growth rates accelerated, from an average of 3.1 percent in 2000 to 6.1 percent by 2007. Against this favorable economic backdrop and the heightened focus on education, SSA countries' primary school completion rate rose by 15 percentage points, on average, between 2000 and 2007 (UN 2009), a remarkable feat considering the continent's rapid population growth. Enrollments at the other levels also rose by impressive margins, albeit from much lower initial levels of coverage.

These salutary trends notwithstanding, a realization is emerging that universalizing primary education will not be sufficient to help sustain SSA's rapid economic growth. The World Bank's Africa Action Plan (World Bank, forthcoming) notes "the need to equip the workforce in African countries with the skills, particularly in science, technology and innovation, to help businesses compete successfully in the global economy." The United Nations (2009) affirms the importance of broadening the scope of concern beyond primary education to encompass the full set of EFA goals. The need to strengthen post-primary education, including technical and vocational education and training, was also emphasized at various recent international meetings, including the 2008 Biennale of the Association of for the Development of Education in Africa (ADEA); the 2009 United

Nations Educational, Scientific, and Cultural Organization (UNESCO) World Conference on Higher Education and the 2009 Conference for Ministers of Finance and of Education hosted by the World Bank, the African Development Bank, and ADEA to discuss options for sustaining the education momentum in Africa amid the current global financial crisis.

The challenge of developing post-primary education is not one of demand. In fact, enrollments have grown so rapidly that they outstrip funding availability, and the resulting imbalance has seriously eroded the quality of services (Brossard and Foko 2007) and crowded out funding for tertiary education and research (World Bank, forthcoming). These problems are starkly obvious in countries such as Burkina Faso, Cameroon, Côte d'Ivoire, Guinea, Kenya, Mali, Mauritius, and Togo, where higher education enrollments have grown three times faster than public spending on this subsector between 1991 and 2006 (World Bank, forthcoming). In countries where overall spending on education already absorbs a sizable share of total public spending, the need for a sectorwide strategy to rationalize spending across the whole sector and improve its efficiency is probably unavoidable and may be very beneficial. In all settings, such a holistic approach may help to create a virtuous cycle by ensuring that scarce resources are used to equip the workforce with skills that can help sustain and accelerate economic growth, so that growth in turn can generate the resources for further deepening the investments in education.

A holistic approach that takes into account all subsectors of the education and training system has become even more relevant in the context of the current global economic downturn. Although data are not yet available to fully assess its impact, the financial crisis is likely to make it more difficult to mobilize funding for education from domestic as well as external sources (UN 2009). At the same time, preliminary figures suggest that foreign direct investment and remittances to SSA countries have already started falling (IMF 2009). Despite continued expressions of donor commitments to the Millennium Development Goals (MDGs), the emergence of new global priorities—including climate change, food security, and pandemics—and a greater concern about countries' macroeconomic stability may weaken rather than strengthen the education sector's claim on external aid in the coming years (AFD 2009). Because resources are fungible, the amount of aid earmarked for education may be less important than the amounts that governments budget for education, including how they allocate the budget across subsectors. In a resource-constrained environment, the challenge is to find the best outcome for the sector as a whole. The analytical approach proposed in this book—centering on a unified and internally coherent simulation model that incorporates policy choices relating to quantity and quality for all key subsectors—is a tool designed to help in this regard. The results presented here are by no means comprehensive; they are intended instead to illustrate the nature of the policy choices and tradeoffs that policy makers face. Ideally, the tool would be adapted to country-specific contexts and used to generate timely inputs relevant to dialogue at the country level.

CHAPTER 3

Methodology and Data

Countries in Sub-Saharan Africa (SSA) are highly diverse in the many dimensions that describe an education system. These dimensions include, for example, the structure and organization of the education system, the initial coverage of the different levels of education, the volume of domestic resources (public and private) mobilized for the sector, the degree of dependence on external aid, the way services are delivered, and the pattern of spending per student across types and levels of education (World Bank, forthcoming). In view of the diversity of these dimensions, the analytical approach in this study entails building a simulation model around a common structural framework that also leaves room for adaptation to country-specific conditions.[1] In essence, the simulation results are an aggregation of country-specific results generated on the basis of data for each of the SSA countries included in the study.

As an analytical tool, the simulation model can easily compute any number of permutations of policies. The focus here, however, is on a limited number of simulations whose results are intended to illustrate key tradeoffs, to identify the scope of possible options, to point out policy choices that are promising and thus worthy of further exploration, to quantify the financing gap implied in each policy scenario, and to evaluate the overall coherence and sustainability of subsector policies when considered as a package for the whole system.

The base-year data for the simulations have been culled from various sources. These sources include the large number of education country status reports[2] prepared thus far by the World Bank, often in collaboration with the Pôle de Dakar, United Nations Educational, Scientific, and Cultural Organization (UNESCO) Regional Office for Education (BREDA); public expenditure reviews prepared by the World Bank; data used in previous education sector simulation models of the World Bank and those of

UNESCO; data supplied by UNESCO Institute of Statistics (UIS);[3] and institutional databases maintained by the World Bank (such as EdStats[4]) and the International Monetary Fund (for macroeconomic and public finance indicators). Because of the large number of countries involved and because each variable in the simulation model must share the same definition across countries, it proved impossible to compile the requisite base-year data for the same base-year for all countries. Thus, depending on data availability, the base year fell between 2000 and 2005. The time horizon for the simulation is fixed at 2020 for all countries.

NOTES

1. See the background volume for more details of the specification of the parameters of the simulation model and how the country-specific features are embedded in the model.

2. Most education country status reports can be found at either http://www.worldbank.org/afr/education or http://go.worldbank.org/4Z2L1R94O0.

3. UIS data on education are available online at http://www.uis.unesco.org.

4. EdStats can be accessed online at http://www.worldbank.org/education/edstats.

CHAPTER 4

The Pressure of Rising Enrollment

To contextualize the discussion, the data in table 4.1 show the current status of enrollment coverage by level of education on average for the 33 countries included in the study. For illustrative purposes, the table also includes data for a few specific countries.[1] Three features are noteworthy in the table:

- The SSA region remains far from achieving universal primary school completion.
- The coverage of secondary education is comparatively low in SSA.
- The variation in education coverage across countries in SSA is very large at all levels of education.

Primary school completion is still far from being universal in SSA, averaging only 52 percent across the 33 countries around the mid-2000s. Although completion rates have risen much more rapidly since 1999 than in the past—at 1.7 percentage points a year compared to only 0.1 points a year during 1990–99—continuation at this rate implies that SSA's primary school completion rate in 2015 would be only 68 percent instead of the Millennium Development Goal of 100 percent by that date (World Bank, forthcoming).

Coverage of post-primary education in SSA is also modest in absolute terms as well as compared with such education in low-income countries in other parts of the world. Barely two-thirds of primary school leavers make the transition to lower secondary education, compared to about 80 percent in low-income countries in Asia.[2] While only 33 and 14 percent of the relevant age groups enroll in the lower and upper secondary cycles, respectively, in low-income SSA, the corresponding figures are around 55 and 30 percent in low-income Asian countries. Coverage in tertiary education averages 323 students per 100,000 inhabitants in low-income SSA, compared to about 900 per 100,000 inhabitants in low-income Asian countries.

Table 4.1 Educational Coverage in Sub-Saharan Africa by Level of Education, Circa 2005

Country (base year)	Primary	Lower secondary		Upper secondary		TVET	Tertiary
	Primary completion rate (%)	Transition rate P–S1 (%)	Gross intake rate (%)	Transition rate S1–S2 (%)	Gross intake rate (%)	Share of secondary enrollment (%)	Students per 100,000 inhabitants
Burkina Faso (2004)	31	58	18	44	4.2	9	201
Cameroon (2003)	60	55	33	65	18.7	23	494
Mali (2004)	42	81	33	40	8.4	10	284
Niger (2002)	22	66	14	40	2.2	3	51
Nigeria (2005)	76	52	40	83	28.3	1	1,188
Rwanda (2003)	46	35	16	78	10.7	11	252
Tanzania (2002)	60	28	16	30	2.0	<1	84
Zambia (2005)	73	62	45	41	16.0	2	218
Average of 33 countries	52.2	63.1	33.1	58.2	13.7	8.8	323

Source: Appendix table B.1.
Note: P: primary, S1: lower secondary, S2: upper secondary.

Significant variation in educational coverage occurs across SSA countries at all levels. The primary school completion rate varies, for example, from 22 percent in Niger to nearly 80 percent in Nigeria, while the share of the age group with access to lower secondary education varies from 16 percent in Rwanda to 45 percent in Zambia. The diversity in coverage is even greater in higher education, with the number of students per 100,000 inhabitants ranging from around 50 in Niger to nearly 1,200 in Nigeria. The great diversity across countries implies that, while regional averages are a convenient summary statistic, they are an inadequate basis for generalizations about education in Sub-Saharan Africa.

ENROLLMENT GROWTH IN PRIMARY EDUCATION

The pressure on post-primary education depends on demographic factors[3] and the pace of progress toward universal primary completion. Because initial primary school completion rates are still relatively low and fertility rates remain high in most SSA countries (Lam 2007), the projected number of primary school completers in 2020 is expected to be sizable. For example, if all SSA countries attained a primary completion rate of 95 percent by 2020, the 33 SSA countries in this study would have a total of 22.2 million primary school completers in 2020, compared to 9.4 million around 2005, an increase by a factor of 2.4 over the period (table 4.2).

Table 4.2 Primary School Completion Rates and Number of Pupils Completing the Cycle, Circa 2005 and Projected in 2020

Country (base year)	Primary completion rate (%)		Number of students completing the primary cycle (thousands)		
	Base year	2020	Base year	2020	Ratio 2020/ base year
Burkina Faso (2004)	31	95	106	514	4.8
Cameroon (2003)	60	95	231	439	1.9
Mali (2004)	42	95	144	533	3.7
Niger (2002)	22	95	69	574	8.3
Nigeria (2005)	76	95	2,595	4,135	1.6
Rwanda (2003)	46	95	112	295	2.6
Tanzania (2002)	60	95	555	1,096	2.0
Zambia (2005)	73	95	227	367	1.6
Avg. 33 countries	52.2	95.0	9,355	22,235	3.0[a]– 2.4[b]

Source: Appendix table B.1.
Note: a. Unweighted average
b. average weighted by school-age population in the different countries.

The country-specific projections in the table reveal a mixed picture, with the projected increase over the period ranging from a factor of no more than 2 in such countries as Cameroon, Nigeria, and Zambia, to a factor of about 5 in Burkina Faso, to a factor greater than 8 in Niger. These data suggest that the effort required to universalize primary school completion will differ considerably from country to country; correspondingly, the pressure on lower secondary education in the next 15 years or so will also be more intense in some countries than others.

IMPACT OF PRIMARY SCHOOL COMPLETION ON LOWER SECONDARY EDUCATION

The expanding pool of primary school completers will inevitably put pressure on subsequent levels of education, beginning with lower secondary education. How intense the pressure will be depends on the rate of transition between the primary and lower secondary cycles. Table 4.3 offers some perspective in this regard. In the initial year (around 2005), there were 14.9 million students enrolled in lower secondary education in our sample of 33 SSA countries. If primary school completion rates rose to

Table 4.3 Potential Growth in Lower Secondary Enrollments by Country

| | Base year | | | 2020 | | | | |
| | | | | Base-year transition rate maintained | | | 100% transition | |
	Transition rate P-S1 %	Gross intake rate to lower secondary (%)	Lower secondary enrollm. (thousands)	Gross intake rate to lower secondary (%)	Lower secondary enrollm. (thousands)	Ratio 2020/ base year enrollm.	Enrollm. in lower secondary (thousands)	Ratio 2020/base year enrollm.
Burkina Faso (2004)	58	18	231	55	1,078	4.7	1,859	8.1
Cameroon (2003)	56	32	560	52	945	1.7	1,718	3.1
Mali (2004)	81	33	347	77	1,186	3.4	1,474	4.2
Niger (2002)	66	14	148	63	1,370	9.3	2,075	14.1
Nigeria (2005)	52	40	3,706	50	6,212	1.7	11,850	3.2
Rwanda (2003)	35	16	117	34	290	2.5	821	7.0
Tanzania (2002)	28	16	454	27	1,194	2.6	4,265	9.4
Zambia (2005)	62	45	271	59	437	1.6	705	2.6
Avg. 33 countries	63.1	33.1	14,909	59.9	37,228	3.5*– 2.5**	62,934	6.1[a]– 4.2[b]

Source: Appendix table B.2
Note: a. Unweighted average
b. average weighted by school-age population in the different countries.

95 percent by 2020 and the rates of primary-to-lower-secondary transition were maintained at current levels in each country, the number of students in lower secondary education would be 37.2 million by 2020—an increase by a factor of 2.5 over current levels. If all primary school completers were allowed to continue on to lower secondary education, enrollments in the lower secondary cycle would rise to 62.9 million by 2020, an increase by a factor of 4.2 over the period.

As expected, SSA countries face diverse prospects in terms of pressure on lower secondary education. With unchanged transition rates between primary and lower secondary education, the projected number of students in lower secondary education in 2020 relative to the number in the base year varies from less than 1.5 times in Lesotho and Zimbabwe; to around 3.0 times in Mali, Rwanda, and Tanzania; to more than 6.0 times in Mozambique; and to as high as 9.0 times in Niger. If the transition rate were raised to 100 percent, the corresponding multiples would be much higher and more diverse across countries: around 2.0 times in Lesotho, Togo, and Zimbabwe; close to 4.0 times in Guinea and Mali; around 9.0 times in Burundi, Tanzania, and Uganda; and more than 11.0 times in Mozambique and Niger.

Some of the 33 SSA countries will be able to cope better than others with the projected increase in enrollment in lower secondary education. The following cutoff points provide one way to separate the countries into three groups according to the logistical challenges[4] posed by the projected increase in lower secondary enrollments in 2020:

- A ratio no higher than 2.0 relative to base year enrollments indicates that the projected increase is probably feasible to handle.
- A ratio between 2.0 and 3.5 indicates that it presents a real challenge.
- A ratio exceeding 3.5 indicates that it is poses great difficulties.

These benchmarks provide the typology shown in table 4.4. Only five countries in the sample—Republic of Congo, Ghana, Lesotho, Togo, and Zimbabwe—fall into the first group, because both primary school completion rates and transition rates between the primary and secondary cycles are already high in the base year. The large majority of the countries fall into the third category, among them Burkina Faso, Burundi, Chad, Central African Republic, Guinea-Bissau, Madagascar, Mali, Mauritania, Mozambique, Niger, and Uganda. For these countries, even the goal of maintaining the current rate of transition between primary and lower secondary education—in the face of progress toward universal primary school completion by 2020—presents practically insurmountable logistical challenges.

Table 4.4 Potential Logistic Difficulties for Countries to Achieve Two Lower Secondary Education Coverage Goals by 2020

		Logistic aspect of achieving near universal lower secondary education		
		Fairly easy	Fairly difficult	Very difficult
Logistic aspect of achieving the goal of maintaining the current primary-secondary transition rate	Fairly easy	Congo, Rep. Ghana Lesotho Togo Zimbabwe	Cameroon Côte d'Ivoire Nigeria Zambia	Malawi
	Fairly difficult		Benin Congo, Dem. Rep. Eritrea The Gambia	Ethiopia Guinea Rwanda Senegal Sierra Leone Tanzania
	Very difficult			Burkina Faso Burundi Chad Central African Republic Guinea-Bissau Madagascar Mali Mauritania Mozambique Niger Uganda

Source: Authors' construction based on data in appendix table B.2.
Note: Kenya and Sudan are not included because they have 8-year primary cycles and no lower secondary cycle.

The logistical scale of expanding the number of lower secondary places is obviously only one aspect of challenges to developing appropriate policies for post-primary education. Decision makers face similar concerns about numbers at the other levels as well. Beyond the numbers, the financial implications of alternative paths for expansion under various options for organizing provision of services also matter in policy development. The discussion herein examines the options in greater detail, using the simulation model described previously to quantify their implications. The simulation assumptions correspond to policy choices that fall under three main rubrics:

- coverage of the education system by level and type of education
- the quality and organization of services
- the division between public and private financing of services.

These assumptions are explained in later chapters, followed by an analysis of the financial implications of various combinations of the assumptions, providing a sectorwide perspective on the policy options.[5]

NOTES

1. Data on all 33 countries can be found in appendix table 1.

2. Afghanistan, Bangladesh, Cambodia, the Democratic Republic of Korea, Lao PDR, Myanmar, Nepal, Pakistan, Papua New Guinea, Solomon Islands, and Vietnam.

3. Appendix table B.6 provides the rates of demographic growth used in the projections.

4. These include building additional classrooms or recruiting and training new teachers.

5. Although the simulation model can compute any number of policy combinations, only selected scenarios are presented, sufficient to illustrate the range of possible options without overwhelming the reader.

CHAPTER 5

Coverage of Post-Primary Education

D etermining the quantitative coverage of the system is a logical first step in shaping policies for developing post-primary education. Two approaches are available to guide the choices. One approach assumes a model of continuity between cycles of education. It corresponds to the idea that the curriculum at each level of schooling is meant to equip students for the next level and that parents want their children to go as far as possible in their formal education. In this somewhat laissez-faire picture, the number of entrants to a given level of education—hence the corresponding extent of coverage—is deduced simply by applying the current (or an assumed target) rate of transition between the two cycles concerned to the number of students enrolled in the last grade of the previous cycle. The second approach assumes a model of discontinuity in the pattern of student flow. It responds to the fact that, in many Sub-Saharan African (SSA) countries, employment opportunities in the formal or modern sector of the economy are limited and likely to remain so in the foreseeable future. Also, in most of these countries, the labor market is already saturated with large numbers of unemployed secondary and tertiary graduates. In this setting, taking proactive measures to regulate and diversify the pattern of student flow would help prevent an unsustainable buildup of frustration among jobless, educated youth as well as improve efficiency in the use of public funds (Brossard and Foko 2007).

In this chapter, we use the simulation model to compare the implications for enrollment growth corresponding to various degrees of continuity (or, conversely, discontinuity) in the management of student flow. The simulation results are presented following an explanation of the simulation assumptions and a discussion of the factors that may inform the decisions of policymakers.

SIMULATION ASSUMPTIONS IN STUDENT FLOW MANAGEMENT

As in most simulation models, our model allows for choices pertaining to enrollments at the following specific levels and types of educational options:

- primary education
- lower secondary education
- upper secondary education
- school-to-work transition programs
- technical and vocational education and training (TVET)
- tertiary education.

The addition of school-to-work transition programs is an important feature in the simulation model in that it makes it possible to simulate the implications of explicit strategies for diversifying educational options at both the post-primary and post-secondary levels.[1]

Five scenarios of student flow are used to illustrate the range of enrollment growth by level and type of program, with 2020 as the end date for the simulations. In brief, their distinguishing assumptions are as follows:[2]

- **Scenario ES-1** corresponds to a situation in each of the 33 SSA countries where (1) the primary completion rate rises from the level in the base year to 95 percent by 2020, (2) all primary school completers go on to lower secondary school and 10 percent among them enroll in TVET programs, (3) the transition rate from lower secondary to the upper secondary cycle remains as in the base year and 15 percent of the upper secondary students enroll in TVET programs, (4) half of the students who complete lower secondary education exit to the labor market via a school-to-work transition program, and (5) the transition rate between upper secondary and tertiary education remains the same as in the base year.
- **Scenario ES-2** is comparable to scenario ES-1 in all respects, except that only 80 percent rather than 100 percent of the primary school completers continue on to the lower secondary cycle and 15 percent among them enroll in TVET programs, and half of the remaining primary school completers exit to the labor market via a school-to-work transition program.
- **Scenario ES-3** marks a shift from the previous two scenarios by making a distinct separation between the lower levels of the system (primary and lower secondary education) and the upper levels (upper secondary and tertiary education). TVET and school-to-work

transition programs both have lower and upper level components, as in the other scenarios. The simulation first derives the target enrollment in tertiary education from a regression analysis of the relation between coverage at this level of education and the level of graduate unemployment[3]; for the purpose of this scenario, the target rate of unemployment is set at 25 percent. In turn, the number of students in upper secondary education is computed simply by multiplying the cohort size in tertiary education by a factor of 2.5, the latter an optional value chosen to simulate a reasonable number of pupils entering the labor market at this stage. In addition, the scenario assumes that 25 percent of upper secondary students are enrolled in TVET programs. For the lower levels, the assumptions are the same as in ES-2, implying near universal access to schooling up to the lower secondary cycle. Reconciling this implication with the restricted enrollments in the upper secondary cycle means that a proportion of lower secondary school leavers will not go beyond this level of schooling. The simulation assumes that all of these school leavers will exit to the labor market via a school-to-work transition program.

- **Scenario ES-4** is similar to ES-3, except that it is more restrictive on three counts: (1) the share of primary school leavers transitioning to the lower secondary cycle declines from 80 percent to 65 percent; (2) the share of lower secondary school leavers who benefit from school-to-work transition programs falls from 100 percent to 50 percent; and (3) the number of places in tertiary education is made consistent with an unemployment rate of 20 percent instead of 25 percent (implying fewer places at this level of education than in scenario ES-3).

- **Scenario ES-5** introduces the option of altering the structural organization of primary and secondary schooling. Keeping unchanged the total duration of these cycles, the simulation allows for a 9-year cycle of basic education, followed by a single cycle of secondary education of the relevant residual duration. Two reasons motivate consideration of this scenario: (1) the complementary nature of primary and lower secondary schooling and the fact that most SSA governments have expressed a desire to universalize basic education, and (2) the greater scope for managing the cost of service delivery, as will be explored in a later chapter. For the simulation results presented below, the calculations assume that completion rates in the 9-year basic education cycle would reach 80 percent by 2020. The parameters for upper secondary and tertiary education are the same as in ES-4. There would no longer be a lower secondary TVET sector because it would be absorbed into the 9-year basic cycle.

CHOOSING OPTIONS FOR STUDENT FLOW MANAGEMENT

The five simulation scenarios range from models of continuity (scenarios ES-1 and ES-2) for managing student flow, to models of discontinuity (ES-3 and ES-4) and to a model of structural change (ES-5). As education systems in SSA countries mature and as the countries make progress toward universal primary schooling, the last three options become increasingly pertinent as issues of fiscal sustainability come to the fore. Each option assumes that explicit choices are made about the placement of selection points beyond primary education, about cohort sizes and selection criteria and mechanisms at each gateway, and about diversifying the pathways for school-to-work transitions. The advantage of this approach is that explicit choices in these dimensions can bring a strategic, coherent, and proactive perspective to policy design for the whole sector.

In considering the relevance of the various options, three factors are particularly useful to bear in mind:

- **The structural duality of SSA economies**. In most of the SSA countries, a predominant share of the working population—as much as 90 percent, on average—is employed in agriculture and the informal sector (Fields 2007; World Bank, forthcoming; Walther 2006). The percentage employed in the formal or modern sector is modest and has remained unchanged between 1990 and 2003 at about 10 percent of the workforce. The prospects of a significant and rapid shift in this dual structure are modest, at least in the short run, implying that the number of modern sector jobs is likely to grow only slowly.
- **The orientation of educational options at system's upper levels**. In most SSA countries, the options are limited and are typically geared toward preparing graduates for modern sector jobs. For the relatively few who actually secure such jobs, their advanced training may confer significant value; the rest of the school leavers or graduating class must settle for other jobs in the informal sector where such training may be less valued (Kingdon and Soderbom 2008; Fasih 2008).
- **The social returns on investment in education in SSA countries**. The pattern typically suggests that investments at the lower levels of the system (up to lower secondary education) are generally more efficient at generating social benefits than investments at the higher levels.

These patterns are particularly striking for girls' education, as house-hold data from a large number of SSA countries reveal (Cohen and Bloom 2006; World Bank, forthcoming). They suggest that as a mother's educational attainment rises beyond lower secondary edu-cation, the marginal gain per dollar invested tends to diminish sharply in terms of the impact on social welfare, as reflected in such indicators as incidence of poverty, ability to read as an adult, health and childcare behaviors, and child mortality.

Taking these factors into consideration suggests a strategy for man-aging student flow that recognizes the possible necessity—indeed the desirability—of distinguishing between the lower and upper levels of the education system and of diversifying the curricula to facilitate young people's transition to the world of work (Walther and Filipiak 2008; World Bank 2008, forthcoming). At the lower levels of the system, the aim would be to universalize access, while at the upper levels the size of enrollments would be geared toward the absorptive capacity of the labor market. The five simulation scenarios correspond to varying degrees of distinction between the cycles: the sharper the distinction, the more selective the transition between the lower and upper levels of the system. The implications for enrollments in 2020 under each of the simulation scenarios are presented below. These results set the stage for analyzing, in the final chapter of this paper, the fiscal implications of the various policy options.

PROJECTED ENROLLMENT IN 2020 UNDER ALTERNATIVE OPTIONS FOR STUDENT FLOW MANAGEMENT

The aggregate picture of 2020 projected enrollment, based on the sim-ulation results for each of the 33 SSA countries in the sample, is shown in table 5.1. For primary education, the first four simulation scenarios—ES-1 to ES-4—assume a primary school completion rate of 95 percent by 2020. Thus, in all four scenarios, the aggregate number of primary school pupils is expected to rise from 100.4 million in the base year, to 161.0 million by 2020, an increase by a factor of 1.6. Under scenario ES-5, where basic education is extended to 9 years and the completion rate is assumed to be 80 percent, total enrollment is projected to reach 211.6 million in 2020, an increase by a multiple of 1.85 over base-year enrollments in the primary and lower secondary cycles. These results suggest that the base of the system will continue to experience very substantial growth in numbers in the coming decade.

ST. MARY'S UNIVERSITY COLLEGE
A COLLEGE OF THE QUEEN'S UNIVERSITY OF BELFAST

Table 5.1 Simulation Results: Student Enrollments by Level of Education in 2020 for 33 Low-Income SSA Countries
million

Year	Coverage scenario	Transition rate P–S1 (%)	Transition beyond S1	Primary	Lower secondary			Upper secondary			Tertiary
					General	TVET	School-to-work transition program	General	TVET	School-to-work transition program	
	Base year	63	–	100.4	13.8	n/a	n/a	7.2	n/a	n/a	3.0
2020	ES-1	100	"Continuity"		56.6	5.7	0.0	25.8	3.5	2.7	13.8
	ES-2	80		161.0	42.8	6.9	2.0	20.4	2.7	2.1	10.8
	ES-3	80	"Discontinuity"		42.8	6.9	2.0	5.8	1.5	9.5	3.1
	ES-4	65			32.7	7.5	3.4	5.4	0.8	3.8	2.5
	ES-5	9 years of primary	"Discontinuity"	211.6		0.0	0.0	5.8	0.8	7.5	2.5

Notes: Rate of real growth of per capita GDP: 2% per year.
n/a: not available. P: primary, S1: lower secondary, S2: upper secondary.
Appendix E provides the corresponding simulation results for each of the 33 countries.
Appendix D provides the aggregate simulation results corresponding to real per capita GDP growth of 0% and 2% per year.

Projections of enrollments in 2020 for the other levels and types of programs vary considerably under the various scenarios. Not surprisingly, they are highest under ES-1 for all segments of the post-primary system, an outcome fully consistent with the scenario's assumptions of universal transition from the primary to the lower secondary cycle and of perpetuation of current rates of transition beyond the lower secondary cycle. The most striking result is the difference in the projected enrollments between two sets of simulations, one set consisting of ES-1 and ES-2, and the other ES-3, ES-4, and ES-5. To recall, the first set corresponds to a model of continuity in student flow management, while the second set corresponds to a model of discontinuity in which progression beyond the lower secondary cycle is calibrated to the absorptive capacity of the modern sector of the labor market. In the first set of projections, enrollments in 2020 in tertiary education, for example, would rise by a factor of 3.6 and 4.6 relative to the base year; in the second set, the increase would be by a factor of between 1.1 and 1.5.

To gain an overall perspective on the growth in enrollments, consider the projected aggregate for all segments of the system beyond the primary cycle. In the base year, the aggregate enrollment was 24.4 million for the 33 SSA countries in the sample. By 2020, the number could reach 59 to 108 million, an increase of 2.4 to 4.5 times the enrollments in the base year. Thus, even under the most selective scenario (ES-4), the increase is significant and will pose very demanding logistical challenges. In ES-5, where a 9-year basic education cycle is introduced to integrate primary and lower secondary education into a single cycle, the projected enrollments are comparable to those in scenario ES-4. The main difference between these two scenarios relates to costs, a topic considered in greater detail in later chapters.

NOTES

1. The characteristics of these programs are discussed in a later chapter. For the purpose of the current chapter, the focus is on the number of students that might be involved.

2. Appendix table C.1 provides a schematic summary of the five coverage options.

3. The regression is documented in World Bank, forthcoming. This feature in the model implies that in scenarios where enrollments in tertiary education are linked to the level of per capital GDP and the unemployment rate, the projections will be sensitive to the assumed rate of economic growth. This expectation would apply to scenarios ES-3 as well as ES-4 and ES-5, but not to ES-1 and ES-2. Similarly, since enrollments in upper secondary education are derived from the projected enrollments in tertiary education, this feature in the simulation model also affects the number of students projected in upper secondary education.

6

The Quality and Reach of Educational Services and Related Unit Costs

High-quality educational services are a desirable goal, but they are costly to provide. In countries facing severe financial constraints, these services inevitably would be available to relatively few people. Therefore, for the system as a whole, compromises must be struck between providing educational services that meet acceptable standards for quality and reaching as many of the target populations as desired. The challenge is to determine what those standards are, bearing in mind that what one country deems "acceptable" may not qualify as such in another country. For the purpose of this report, the focus is on the quality of services from the perspective of inputs, given its direct link to costs and resource needs. The larger issue of how well resources are transformed into learning outcomes is also important—perhaps critically so, given that enhancing student learning is a key goal of educational policy—but it requires a separate analysis not attempted here.[1] The discussion in this chapter first documents the diversity in the delivery of educational services across SSA countries. It then proposes reference benchmarks for the simulation model in terms of "acceptable" standards for the quality of services from an input perspective. The discussion also explains two features embedded in the simulation model, one to respond to the fact that some of the simulation parameters (such as teacher salaries) are sensitive to a country's level of per capita gross domestic product (GDP), and the second to allow for a pattern of rising marginal costs as educational services are extended to rural populations.

CURRENT PATTERNS OF PER-STUDENT PUBLIC SPENDING BY LEVEL OF EDUCATION

Table 6.1 shows average per-student public spending in our sample of 33 low-income Sub-Saharan African (SSA) countries; for comparison, it also includes the relevant data for three other groups of developing

Table 6.1   Public Spending per Student by Level of Education, Sub-Saharan Africa and Other Country Groups, Circa 2005

| | Per-student spending in percentage of GDP per capita | | | | | | |
| | Primary (%) | Secondary | | | | Tertiary | |
		Lower secondary (%)	Upper secondary (%)	Average (%)	Ratio secondary/ primary	Tertiary (%)	Ratio tertiary/ primary
Low-income countries[a]							
Sub-Saharan Africa	11	33	60	40	3.7	370	34
Other regions	11	–	–	12	1.1	53	5
Middle-income countries[b]							
Sub-Saharan Africa	15	–	–	27	1.8	200	13
Other regions	14	–	–	15	1.1	34	2

Sources: Data for low-income SSA are from the database compiled for this study. Data for other countries and regions are from UIS and EdStats.
Note: See also appendix table B.3–appendix table B.5 for more details about school organization and per-student spending.
a. Countries eligible for lending from the International Development Association (IDA).
b. Countries eligible for lending from the International Bank for Reconstruction and Development (IBRD).
Dash = data not available.

countries in Africa and elsewhere. Relative to per capita GDP, the level of public spending per student in SSA countries averages 11 percent for primary education, 40 percent for secondary education, and 370 percent for tertiary education. For middle-income SSA countries, the corresponding figures are 15 percent, 27 percent, and 200 percent; and for low-income countries outside SSA, they are 11 percent, 12 percent, and 53 percent. These comparisons are a first indication that the cost structure of post-primary education in SSA countries is likely to pose a serious impediment to its expansion and development.

A closer look at the data on public spending per student reveals the following noteworthy features:

- In **primary** education, the figure for SSA countries is comparable to the averages for the other country groups, generally falling in the range of 11 to 15 percent of per capita GDP.
- In **secondary** education, SSA countries' average in upper secondary is nearly twice as high as in lower secondary: 60 percent of per capita GDP compared to 33 percent.[2] The average for the two cycles, at 40 percent of per capita GDP, is more than 3 times the average for low-income countries in other parts of the developing world. Across SSA countries, public spending per student in secondary education is, on average, about 3.7 as high as in primary education.

- In **tertiary** education, SSA countries' average is substantially greater than the average for lower levels in the system, and it is also much higher than the averages in other country groups. On average, SSA countries spend 34 times as much on each student in tertiary education as on a pupil in primary school; the corresponding ratio is 5 times in low-income countries outside SSA and 13 times in middle-income SSA countries.

The generally high levels of public spending per student in secondary and especially in tertiary education set African education systems apart from those of other countries. They are one reason the coverage of post-primary education in the region remains relatively modest today and why expanding it will pose significant challenges in the coming years. To relieve this constraint on expansion, one must understand the underlying drivers of SSA countries' high level of spending per student. Because the bulk of expansion in the coming decade will be in secondary education, understanding the cost drivers in secondary education is especially important. This issue is considered in greater detail below.

COMPARATIVE PERSPECTIVES ON COST DRIVERS IN SECONDARY EDUCATION

How much teachers are paid, how their instructional time is used, and how much is spent on complementary inputs are important drivers of per-student spending. These variables are therefore the main loci of policy decision making. To evaluate the options in this regard, a key challenge is to identify appropriate benchmarks that would correspond to reasonable input standards for service delivery.

To explore these issues, one may find it helpful to consider first the data on the key cost drivers in table 6.2, which, for reasons of space, shows only the average for all the 33 SSA countries in the sample and the corresponding figures for selected countries in the sample.[3] A striking feature is that the regional average masks highly diverse arrangements for service delivery. The average number of students per class can vary from fewer than 20 to more than 80; the average teacher's pay relative to the per capita GDP can go from a multiple of 2 to a multiple of more than 9; and spending on inputs other than teachers as a share of total recurrent spending can range from 15 to 60 percent. The great diversity across countries suggests that no fixed organizational arrangements can be implied by such generic terms as "lower secondary" or "upper secondary" education; alternatively stated, countries do enjoy substantial scope in choosing how services are organized and delivered.

Table 6.2   Characteristics and Costs of School Organization in Secondary Education

	Average teacher salary (in multiples of GDP/capita)	Students per teacher (1)	Students per class (2)	Teachers per class (ratio (2)/(1))	Share of recurrent expenditure other than for teacher salaries (%)	Per-student spending (in multiples of GDP/capita)
Lower secondary						
Burkina Faso	9.3	50.0	75.0	1.5	60.4	0.47
Burundi	9.3	20.5	42.4	2.1	29.1	0.64
Cameroon	6.5	31.1	40.3	1.3	34.3	0.32
Ethiopia	8.1	48.3	67.8	1.4	18.6	0.21
Guinea	2.9	47.6	88.9	1.9	44.0	0.11
Malawi	7.7	26.3	50.0	1.9	40.0	0.49
Togo	8.7	54.2	87.9	1.6	13.6	0.19
Uganda	7.4	6.8	15.2	2.2	25.1	1.45
Average of 33 countries	6.0	35.5	53.5	1.6	38.0	0.33
Upper secondary						
Burkina Faso	13.0	39.0	52.0	1.3	48.0	0.64
Burundi	11.0	16.4	32.4	2.0	72.0	2.40
Cameroon	6.8	29.1	36.4	1.3	36.5	0.37
Ethiopia	11.9	50.3	81.7	1.6	40.5	0.40
Guinea	2.9	52.3	95.0	1.8	41.0	0.09
Malawi	7.7	26.3	50.0	1.9	40.0	0.49
Togo	9.0	33.3	62.4	1.9	15.9	0.32
Uganda	7.4	6.8	15.2	2.2	25.1	1.45
Average of 33 countries	7.4	27.1	45.7	1.8	39.9	0.60

Source: See appendix table B.3 and appendix table B.4.

Given the considerable spread in the way secondary education is organized, the future development of secondary education is likely to pose fewer problems in some countries than others. In particular, the government's financial burden would be more manageable where current organizational choices already favor modest levels of per-student spending. Yet lower costs in and of themselves are not necessarily optimal if this implies accepting enormous class sizes for teaching and learning, possibly 80 or more students in each class. An important challenge for policy makers, therefore, is to identify suitable benchmarks for the cost drivers in order to set the future development of the subsector on a sustainable path while assuring adequate schooling conditions. The experiences of other developing countries that have achieved sustained growth of their secondary school systems provide some inspiration in this regard.

Table 6.3 contains pertinent comparative data on the main cost drivers. It shows that with regard to student-teacher ratios, the average for SSA (31.4) is comparable to that for low-income countries in other world regions (29.8), but exceeds by a large margin the ratio of about 20 in middle-income countries in Africa and elsewhere. With regard to teacher salaries, the difference between SSA and other countries is particularly striking. Salaries in SSA countries average about 6.0 times the per capita GDP in the lower secondary cycle and 7.4 times in the upper secondary cycle (implying an average of 6.5 times for the two cycles taken together). The corresponding figure is 3.8 in middle-income African countries, 2.8 in low-income non-African countries, and 2.4 in middle-income non-African countries. Thus, when salaries are expressed

Table 6.3 Comparison of Coverage and Organization of Secondary Education, Sub-Saharan Africa and Other Country Groups, Circa 2005

	Context GDP per capita (USD 2003)	GER Lower secondary (%)	GER Upper secondary (%)	Determinants of level of per-student spending Private sector enrollm. as share of total (%)	Share of repeaters (%)	Students/ teacher	Average teacher salary (in multiples of GDP per capita)	Per-student spending (in multiples of GDP per capita)
Low-income countries[a]								
Sub-Saharan Africa	320	32.7	13.8	19.8	13.2	31.4	6.5	0.40
Other regions	734	73.5	46.3	38.6	4.9	29.8	2.8	0.12
Middle-income countries[b]								
Sub-Saharan Africa	3,182	81.6	57.1	21.2	8.8	21.0	3.8	0.27
Other regions	2,477	88.0	58.5	22.4	5.3	19.1	2.4	0.15

Source: Data for low-income SSA are from the database compiled for this study. Data for other countries and regions are from UIS and EdStats.
a. Countries eligible for lending from International Development Association (IDA).
b. Countries eligible for lending from International Bank for Reconstruction and Development (IBRD).

in units of per capita GDP, the average for low-income African countries is 2.4 times as high as that in low-income countries elsewhere in the world. These comparisons of the cost-related variables provide a basis for delimiting the potential values of the cost parameters in the simulation model.

BENCHMARKS FOR COST DRIVERS IN SECONDARY EDUCATION

Benchmarks are useful in the simulation exercise for two main reasons. First, as an alternative to the current values of the cost-drivers, they bring a forward-looking orientation to the evaluation of policy options for cost management. Second, the benchmarks are highly relevant for the 33 low-income SSA countries, given that most, if not all, of them will require external aid to complement domestic resources to attain their educational goals. In this context, having a reference framework helps focus specifically on issues of cost efficiency, thereby providing donor agencies one yardstick, among others, for ensuring that taxpayer money is not being wasted in the education sector. At the same time, the benchmarks provide a basis for treating countries equitably when evaluating appropriate levels of aid and for minimizing the risk of allocating too much to countries with inefficient service delivery arrangements at the expense of countries with more efficient arrangements.

The foregoing considerations motivate an approach similar to that associated with the Education for All Fast Track Initiative (EFA-FTI), which involves specification of indicative benchmarks for an array of cost-sensitive parameters relating to the organization of educational services.[4] To recall, the main purpose of the indicative framework is to provide an objective reference for assessing alternative policy options for the education sector. Its main use is to help focus attention on the most critical structural issues that may impede the sector's future development. As such, the indicative framework is an analytical device, meant as an aid for policy development rather than as a tool for identifying specific conditions to impose on aid-receiving countries.

Because initial conditions and fiscal constraints on the education sector differ widely across the 33 SSA countries in this study, it may be appealing to argue against measuring all the countries against a single reference framework. Yet the diversity across countries is also a strong argument for the use of precisely such a framework, in order to systematize the policy discussions. To reconcile these two perspectives, two indicative frameworks for service delivery in secondary education are developed for the simulations. The first might be termed a "generous" or liberal framework, with parameter values that are consistent with relatively favorable conditions for schooling. The second might be called a "spartan" or cost-conscious framework, in which the parameter values correspond to more economical (but still acceptable) schooling conditions. By negotiating between these two sets of benchmarks, the simulation exercise for each country can be customized to its specific context. Naturally, the choice of parameter values has different cost and budget implications.

To characterize these two indicative frameworks, table 6.4 shows the corresponding values of the key variables in the simulation model. They are organized and discussed as follows: (1) the organization of service delivery, as defined by a set of three variables; (2) the level of teacher salaries; (3) the share of spending on non-teacher inputs; and (4) the rate of grade repetition.

ORGANIZATION OF SERVICE DELIVERY

The three pertinent variables are: average class size or the number of students per instructional group, weekly instructional hours received by students, and weekly hours of teaching performed by teachers. These three variables bear an algebraic relation to the student-teacher ratio.[5] But because they correspond to policy levers that decision makers can act upon more directly than the student-teacher ratio, the simulation model

Table 6.4　Indicative Framework for the Organization of Services in Secondary Education

	Lower secondary		Upper secondary	
	"Generous"	"Spartan"	"Generous"	"Spartan"
Organization of service delivery				
Students per class	40	50	40	45
Hours of instruction per week (students)	28	25	30	27
Teaching hours per week (teachers)	18	21	16	18
Students per teacher	25.7	42.0	21.3	30.0
Average teacher salary (multiples of GDP/capita)	5.0	4.6	6.5	5.6
Expenditure other than teacher salary (%)	45	38	50	42
Share of repeaters (%)	10	10	10	10
Per-student spending (in percent of GDP per capita)	35.4	17.7	60.9	32.2

Source: Authors.
Note: This parameter describes the "basic" level of per-student spending before any adjustment for level of wealth, geographic dimension, or stimulation of demand.

seeks inputs of values for these variables rather than for the student-teacher ratio. The model uses the following values of these three variables:

- In the **lower secondary cycle**, the values for the "generous" scenario are as follows: 40 students per class (better than the current SSA average of 54); 28 hours of instruction per week; and 18 hours of teaching per week. With these parameter values, the implied student teacher ratio is 25.7 (compared with the base year SSA average of 35.5). In the "spartan" scenario, the parameter values are: 50 students per class (still better than the current average); 25 hours of instruction per week; and 21 hours of teaching per week. The student-teacher ratio would then be 42.0, which is slightly higher than the SSA average for the lower secondary cycle (35.5) but better than the SSA average of about 46 for the primary cycle.[6] The assumed instructional hours and teaching loads in both scenarios are well within the ranges observed among SSA countries and are reasonable in absolute terms.
- In the **upper secondary cycle**, the parameter values shown in table 6.4 are generally more resource-intensive than in the previous cycle, implying student-teacher ratios of 21.3 under the "generous" scenario and 30.0 under the "spartan" scenario, compared with the current SSA average of 27.1. The assumed class sizes in these scenarios are 40 and 45, respectively, relative to the SSA average of 45.7 in the base year. As in the scenarios for the lower secondary cycle, the assumptions about instructional hours and teaching loads are within the scope of current practices in the sample of 33 countries.

LEVEL OF TEACHER SALARIES

As mentioned, this variable presents a daunting challenge in most SSA countries because of its cost implications. The annual cost of teacher salaries in the lower secondary cycle averages 6.0 times the per capita GDP, while in the upper secondary cycle, it is 7.4 times, giving an average of 6.5 for the two cycles taken together. For comparison, the annual salary cost of lower secondary teachers is only 2.8 times in low-income non-African countries and 2.4 times in middle-income non-African countries. Adjusting the 2.8 and 2.4 ratios to be consistent with income levels in SSA yields a teacher salary cost of around 3.6 times per capita GDP.[7] Current secondary school teacher salaries in SSA are about 80 percent higher than this level. Thus, even with this adjustment for income differences, the absolute value of the implied salary would still be too low (ie, too far from the current situation). To be a realistic policy option in the coming years.

Another approach for choosing values for this variable is to relate it to salaries in primary education. Under the indicative framework of the EFA-FTI, salaries for primary school teachers are benchmarked at 3.5 times the per capita GDP. Assuming that lower secondary school teachers have three more years of schooling than teachers in primary schools, and assuming that the private rate of return to each additional year of schooling is 12 percent—a very reasonable rate—the salary of lower secondary school teachers would be about 40 percent higher, or 4.9 times the per capita GDP. Similarly, if upper secondary school teachers have five more years of schooling than primary school teachers, their salary would be 76 percent higher, or 6.2 times the per capita GDP.[8] Thus, for the simulation exercise, the assumptions about teacher salaries are as follows: in the "generous" scenario, the values are 5 times the per capita GDP for lower secondary and 6.5 times for upper secondary; in the "spartan" scenario, the corresponding ratios are 4.6 and 5.6, respectively.

RECURRENT EXPENDITURE EXCLUDING THE SALARIES OF TEACHERS[9]

The choice of values for this variable in the simulation scenarios is based on the range observed across the 33 SSA countries. On average, expenditure on inputs other than teacher salaries accounts for about 38 percent of total recurrent spending in the lower secondary cycle and 40 percent in the upper secondary cycle. The variance is large around these averages. For the "generous" scenario in the simulations, the assumed value of this variable is 45 percent in lower secondary education and 50 percent in the upper secondary cycle. In the "spartan" scenario, the shares are, respectively, 38 and 42 percent.

REPETITION RATE

This variable does not affect spending per student but does have budget implications in that the higher its value, the more students remain in the system and the greater the budget required to maintain operations. In recent years, repetition rates in SSA countries have been rising and currently average about 13 percent in both cycles of secondary schooling in the 33 SSA countries. The rates are around 5 percent in non-African countries and less than 9 percent in middle-income African countries. For simplicity, the simulation exercise assumes a rate of 10 percent for both cycles of secondary schooling for both the "generous" and "spartan" scenarios.

The level of per-student spending implied by the combinations of policy choices discussed above appears in the last row of the table. Under the "generous" scenario, per-student spending amounts to an average of 0.354 times the per capita GDP in the lower secondary cycle, and an average of 0.609 times in the upper secondary cycle. The corresponding averages for the "spartan" scenario are 0.177 and 0.322 times, respectively. These results suggest that, while schooling conditions are inevitably less comfortable under the "spartan" scenario, the disadvantage is not dramatic, as reflected in the differences between the two scenarios in the values of the variables pertaining to organizational arrangements, the level of teacher salaries and the share of spending on inputs other than teacher salaries.[10] Yet the combined impact of making cost-conscious choices on all three dimensions is substantial: per-student spending under the "spartan" scenario is, on average, only about half as high as that under the "generous" scenario.[11]

COST ASSUMPTIONS FOR TECHNICAL AND VOCATIONAL EDUCATION AND TRAINING

The cost assumptions for technical and vocational education and training (TVET) and higher education (discussed in the next chapter) do not use the in-depth composite approach adopted for lower and upper secondary education. Instead, for simplicity, the cost assumptions are linked through proportional ratio to the cost assumptions in secondary education, and to costs in other countries.

With regard to TVET, the simulation model makes a distinction between two very distinct types of activities: (1) formal courses, typically institution based, that are designed as an alternative to the academic or general stream of studies and (2) life skills training, usually of short duration, that are offered at the end of the primary or lower secondary cycle, mainly to help facilitate young people's transition into the world of work. The latter type of TVET activities serves a dual purpose: (1) to equip young people (most of whom will work in the informal sector of the economy) with practical skills at the start of their working life in hopes of enhancing their labor market productivity and (2) to relieve pressure on the upper levels of the system by offering a positive alternative to young people who might otherwise seek to continue their studies in the formal system.

For the purpose of this simulation exercise, only one set of cost parameters for TVET is maintained. This analytical strategy simplifies the presentation without compromising the main conclusions of the exercise. According to available information (which pertains mainly to the first type of courses discussed above), per-student spending on TVET courses, averaged over the different specializations, is typically about three times as high as spending per student in the general stream. On the basis of this relationship, the simulations assume the following cost structure for formal TVET courses: 1.2 times the per capita GDP for courses offered at the lower secondary level and 1.7 times the per capita GDP for those offered at the upper secondary level.

With regard to the school-to-work transition type of TVET training, cost data are very limited, not least because few countries in fact offer such training at present. For the purpose of the simulation exercise, we made the following cost assumptions: 0.6 times the per capita GDP for courses offered at the end of primary schooling and 0.8 times per capita GDP for those offered at the end of the lower secondary cycle.

COST ASSUMPTIONS FOR HIGHER EDUCATION

The choice of cost benchmarks for the 33 SSA countries encounters two immediate difficulties:

- **SSA's much higher costs relative to the per capita GDP than elsewhere**. For the 33 SSA countries, per-student spending in higher education averages 3.7 times the per capita GDP, compared with 0.54 times in low-income non-African countries and 2.0 times in middle-income SSA countries. These comparisons suggest the presence of Africa-specific cost drivers. While SSA's high costs are neither inevitable nor desirable, it would nonetheless be unrealistic to ignore them entirely in deciding on an appropriate benchmark for the simulation exercise.
- **Highly variable levels of public spending per student across countries**. Among the 33 SSA countries, those with the lowest levels of spending per student probably provide insufficient funding to assure services of a reasonable quality, while those with the highest levels probably have systems that are wasteful. The data for the 33 countries therefore provide an uncertain basis for choosing an appropriate benchmark.

In light of the foregoing observations, a reasonable compromise would be to take the average per-student expenditure in middle-income African countries—that is, 2.0 times the per capita GDP—as a benchmark at which all countries would converge by 2020. This average includes operational costs as well as spending on student welfare services.

In addition to benchmarking the average level of spending per student, the simulation model also differentiates spending by field of study.

For the purpose of this study, three major fields are distinguished: humanities and social sciences; natural sciences; and professional studies[12]. Using available cross-country data, the simulation model assumes the following distribution of enrollment across these three fields: 60 percent, 15 percent, and 25 percent, respectively (table 6.5). Combining this information with available data for the 33 countries on relative cost structures, the simulation assumes the following cost parameters by field of study (in units of per capita GDP): 1.5 times for the humanities and social sciences, 2.4 times the natural sciences, and 2.9 times for professional studies. These assumptions are consistent with the overall average spending of 2.0 times the per capita GDP.

TREATMENT OF CAPITAL COSTS IN THE MODEL

The simulation model also calculates the capital costs in the different scenarios, but only those associated with the construction of classrooms in primary and secondary schools to accommodate growing student enrollments in these cycles. It does not include other capital or development costs, such as those for preschool, teacher training, or higher education. In the model, the capital costs are simply a function of the choice of enrollment scenario (ES-1 to ES-5), the class size, and the unit construction cost.

For class size, a benchmark of 40 students per class is used for primary education; in lower and upper secondary school, a class size of 40 is used in the "generous" option for school organization, while the "spartan" option raises this standard to 50 for lower and 45 for upper secondary schools.[13] Unit construction costs per classroom (furnished and equipped) are $12,000 for primary schools and $16,000 in both lower and upper secondary schools.

Table 6.5 Indicative Framework for the Organization of Services in TVET and Tertiary Education

| | Lower secondary | | Upper secondary | | Tertiary | | | |
	TVET	School-to-work transition program	TVET	School-to-work transition program	Humanities and social sciences	Sciences	Professional studies	Total
Student distribution	–	–	–	–	60%	15%	25%	100%
Unit cost (in multiples of GDP/capita)	1.2	0.6	1.7	0.8	1.5	2.4	2.9	2.0

Source: Authors' construction.

MAKING THE INDICATIVE FRAMEWORK MORE FLEXIBLE

In the context of the Education for All Fast Track Initiative (EFA-FTI), an indicative framework was used to evaluate the cost of attaining the Millennium Development Goal of universalizing primary school completion. Experience with this framework suggests that, while the application of standard benchmarks helped in rationalizing the analysis across a large number of countries, some flexibility in the benchmarks, particularly to take account of differences in countries' level of economic development, might have made the exercise even more useful. The use of a single set of benchmarks proved particularly problematic with regard to teacher salaries—which for primary school teachers were set at an average of 3.5 times the per capita GDP in the FTI framework— and was singled out as particularly problematic in the poorest countries. Where the per capita GDP was $100 or lower, it implied absolute pay levels that in fact fell below the poverty line in many of the countries.

Although this study follows the same practice as the FTI indicative framework in relying on benchmarks—on the argument that it provides a fair basis for evaluating funding gaps for possible external support— important features have been incorporated to make the framework more flexible. In particular, on the cost side, the simulation model allows for adjustments for differences across countries in per capita GDP as well as in population distributions between urban and rural areas, which could affect the cost of service delivery and also require demand-side interventions to enroll the remaining pockets of out-of-school children.[14] These features of flexibility are briefly explained below.

ADJUSTING THE BENCHMARKS FOR TEACHER SALARIES WHERE INCOMES ARE ESPECIALLY HIGH OR LOW

In the simulation exercise, teacher salaries are expressed in units of per capita GDP to avoid the complication of separate assumptions about price inflation over the long time frame of the simulations and also to allow for salary increases as a country grows richer. Analysis of available data on teacher salaries suggests that when expressed in per capita units, this variable bears an inverse relationship to the per capita GDP, even though in absolute terms its value tends to be smaller the poorer the country (see appendix A for further discussion of this point and its implications). This statistical relationship has been used in this simulation exercise to adapt the assumed value of teacher salaries to a country's per capita GDP.

As a result, in the model's primary education module, the value of salaries is benchmarked at 3.0 times per capita GDP for countries with GDP per capita above $600, 3.5 times per capita GDP for countries with GDP in the $300–600 range, and among the latter group, the benchmark is raised to 3.6, 3.9, and 4.2 times the per capita GDP, respectively, when the per capita GDP is $250, $150, and $100 (in 2000 prices). With regard to secondary school teacher salaries, the assumed values for the poorest countries (that is, per capita incomes no higher than $250) are raised by the same proportion above the standard benchmarks attached to the other countries.[15] Similarly, for countries with incomes above $600, lower secondary school teacher salaries (as a multiple of per capita GDP) are lowered as compared with the standard benchmarks.[16]

With regard to TVET and higher education, the simulation model does not specify teacher salaries as a separate variable. Instead, it simply uses spending per pupil as an aggregate variable to reflect the cost of service delivery. For TVET, this variable is pegged to the corresponding variable for secondary education, which therefore implies a built-in adjustment for the poorest countries through the mechanism explained above. For tertiary education, the standard benchmark for per-student spending is 2.0 times the per capita GDP. For the poorest countries, a higher ratio is used that takes into consideration the fact that a large share of the expenditure at this level of education typically goes for inputs that are priced in regional markets (such as academic staff) or even procured in foreign currency and therefore relatively more expensive for the poorest countries (for example, books, computers, and laboratory consumables).[17,18]

ADJUSTING THE BENCHMARKS FOR CURRENT EXPENDITURE, EXCLUDING TEACHER SALARIES

One difficulty in choosing appropriate benchmarks is that this variable covers expenditure denominated in local currency (for example, consumables and salaries of administrative staff) as well as those bought with foreign currency (for example, textbooks). Because this variable is expressed in the simulation model as a share of total unit cost, it is effectively pegged to the level of teacher salaries. Since the latter variable, when expressed in absolute terms, is lower the poorer the country, the implication is that spending on non-salary inputs would also be smaller in absolute terms the lower the income of the country. For the poorest countries, then, the amount thus derived may not be realistic for purchasing inputs on international markets that are required to deliver services of reasonable quality. Thus, for these countries, the amount for non-salary spending is benchmarked at the same absolute amount as countries with a per capita GDP of $300 (in 2000 U.S. dollars).

ADJUSTING FOR THE INCREASING MARGINAL COSTS TO REACH RURAL POPULATIONS

Because universal coverage in primary education, and, increasingly, in lower secondary education, are common goals in many SSA countries, the simulation exercise takes explicit account of the rising marginal costs of reaching rural populations, given that most of the out-of-school population resides in rural areas.[19] The following are two observations about the pattern of enrollments in urban and rural areas in the 33 country sample:

- The **urban share of the school-age population** currently averages about 30 percent in the sample, but its range stretches from less than 20 percent in Burundi and Burkina Faso to about 50 percent in Republic of Congo and The Gambia.
- The **coverage of the education system** is generally much lower in rural than in urban areas at both the primary and lower secondary levels. In lower secondary education, for example, the average gross enrollment ratio is 66.5 percent in urban areas, but only 22.2 percent in rural areas. The pattern of coverage shows the usual wide variation across countries.[20]

These observations and further analysis of the available data imply that among the current out-of-school primary school-age population, about 80 percent on average live in rural areas. The same analysis for the lower secondary cycle suggests an even higher share of 85 percent. While the share does vary around the regional average, the reality is that in all the sample countries, rural residents make up the bulk of the relevant out-of-school populations.

If the goal is to universalize primary and lower secondary schooling, the simulation model must incorporate, in a more explicit manner, the cost of servicing and reaching rural populations. For primary schooling, analysis of economies of scale in service delivery for 16 of the sample countries suggests that per-pupil costs in a school with 100 pupils is on average about 35 percent higher than those in a school with 300 pupils; and it is on average about 25 percent higher in village schools than in city schools. For lower secondary education, economies of scale are more pronounced, with per-student costs in a school with 120 students exceeding by 70 percent those in a school of 400 students. These differences in unit spending among schools of different sizes reflect the impact of fixed costs and the use of specialized teachers who, because of fragmented curricula, cannot fully fill their weekly teaching load in small rural schools. As before, there is substantial variation around these regional averages. In lower secondary education, the difference between schools of 120 and 400 students could be a factor of just 1.15 in some countries to as much as 2.40 in others.[21]

PRIMARY EDUCATION MODULE

For the primary education module in the simulation model, we retained the pupil-teacher ratio at the EFA-FTI indicative benchmark of 40 to 1. A key consideration in doing so is that, given the already large system size in many countries, there should be sufficient room around this average to accommodate, in a pragmatic manner, (slightly) lower ratios in rural or sparsely populated areas while tolerating (slightly) higher ratios in more densely populated areas. By contrast, the simulation exercise raises the benchmark for teacher salaries beyond the FTI indicative value of 3.5 times the per capita GDP. Experience suggests that attracting the remaining out-of-school population typically requires posting teachers to remote rural schools. In practice, teachers may not take up their posts or may fail to turn up regularly to teach their classes without additional incentives. Faced with this difficulty, several SSA countries (for example, The Gambia, Lesotho) have indeed taken measures to address the problem. These measures must obviously target only localities where teacher placement is an issue, and the incentives they provide must be sufficiently large to attract the target teachers. Taking into consideration the experience of countries that have dealt with this challenge, we adapted the benchmarks for salaries by assuming that 15 percent of the teachers in rural areas would require a salary supplement and that the supplement would increase their salaries by an average of 20 percent beyond the standard benchmark. Finally, the simulation exercise makes one other adjustment to take into account the challenges of reaching the remaining out-of-school population as coverage progresses toward the 100 percent mark. Because the relevant population typically consists of the poorest and most tradition-bound segments of society, special efforts to reach them with customized services might be required. The simulation model makes allowance for this possibility by assuming that 10 percent of the rural population falls in this category and that extending primary school coverage to them would entail services that cost 30 percent more than the standard benchmark for per-pupil spending for the rest of the population.

LOWER SECONDARY MODULE

For the lower secondary module in the simulation model, the simulation benchmarks were adjusted only to take account of economies of scale in service delivery; this approach focuses on the source of the rising marginal costs to extend services to rural areas at this level of schooling. To keep costs under control, countries will need to carefully manage two aspects of service delivery simultaneously: (1) the administrative arrangements and pedagogical support functions in small (rural) schools and (2) the curriculum design and the capacity of teachers to teach multiple subjects. While countries clearly differ in their capacity to manage these factors, a key tenet in this study is that some approaches are clearly more efficient and equitable than others and that these should be promoted as the preferred arrangements for expanding coverage in rural areas. Without going into detail on how best to organize educational services in small schools, analysis of existing practices suggests that it is possible, through careful management of staff resources (both teaching and administrative staff), to limit the cost per student in small (rural) schools to no more than 1.3 times that in larger urban schools. For each country, the cost simulations are based on the application of this marginal cost benchmark to the estimated shares of small schools at each point in time.

NOTES

1. Student learning is the subject of a large and continuing research agenda in developed and developing countries alike. The available findings suggest that while schools cannot function without a minimal level of resources, the relation between resources and learning outcomes is weak at best. Important factors that affect performance include the behaviors of key personnel involved in service delivery and the organizational, governance, and management arrangements in the system (Hanushek and Wößmann 2007).

2. For countries outside Sub-Saharan Africa, most of the available data comes from the UNESCO Institute for Statistics. Data from this source do not always make a distinction between the two cycles of secondary education.

3. See appendix table B.3 and appendix table B.4 for data for all 33 SSA countries.

4. The EFA-FTI indicative framework provides benchmarks for seven indicators: government spending on education (about 20 percent of budget), spending on primary education (about 50 percent of education budget), teacher salary (about 3.5 times GDP per capita), pupil-teacher ratio (about 40:1), non-teacher salary spending (33 percent of recurrent spending), average repetition rate (10 percent or lower), and annual hours of instruction (850 or more). See Bruns, Mingat, and Rakotomalala (2003) for details on how these benchmarks were derived.

5. Student-teacher ratio = class size × (teachers' weekly hours of teaching duties/ students' weekly hours instructional time).

6. See appendix table B.5 for data on school organization in primary and tertiary education.

7. Based on a regression between teacher salaries and GDP per capita. The average GDP per capita in low-income SSA countries was $320 in 2003 compared with $734 in low-income countries in other regions.

8. It can also be observed that, in the current situation, a lower secondary school teacher earns 40 percent more on average than a primary school teacher, while the corresponding figure is 70 percent for an upper secondary teacher. Applying these coefficients to the EFA-FTI indicative framework value for primary education, we arrive at a teacher salary level of 4.9 and 6 times the GDP/capita for the two secondary cycles, respectively. These figures are close to those obtained with the other method.

9. This expenditure concerns textbooks, educational materials for students and teachers, water and electricity, upkeep of school buildings and furniture, in-service teacher training, expenditure on administrative and pedagogical support personnel in schools, central and decentralized departments, as well as associated operating expenditures.

10. The effective possibilities of distance education will probably also have to be used.

11. It should also be noted that the indicative framework describes average situations (this is what is important financially), but that its implementation can incorporate relevant modulations around the averages in order to take local or regional specificities into account within each country.

12. Preparing for jobs as professions such as doctor, lawyer, journalist, librarian, or engineer.

13. See also table 6.4.

14. One other feature that might have been added to increase the flexibility of the simulation model pertains to its resource mobilization module. In particular, it would appear appropriate to link a country's ability to mobilize domestic resources through tax revenues to its prospects for economic growth. This expectation is based on the observation that as economies grow and become more formalized, their tax base and capacity to raise revenues also improve. This tendency is borne out by the experience of most countries. However, among the non-oil-producing SSA countries with a per capita GDP below $1,000, the relation is weak at best. A positive and significant relation between per capita GDP and fiscal capacity exists only for more economically mature countries. Thus, in the simulation exercise no adjustment is made to the benchmarks for variables relating to resource mobilization.

15. Appendix A documents the regression behind these assumptions.

16. Appendix E provides the adjusted teacher salaries and unit costs used for each country in the simulations.

17. Per-student spending by field of study is assumed to retain the same relative structure as in table 6.5.

18. Appendix E provides the tertiary unit costs used in the simulations for each country.

19. For upper secondary education, the assumption is that schools will continue to be located mainly in urban areas. This assumption does not apply to lower secondary schools, which must remain close to the populations concerned, particularly with a view to a significant increase in schooling coverage.

20. See, for example, Mingat and Ndem (2008), which work analyses the schooling differences between urban and rural children (but also between girls and boys, rich and poor) at different levels of education in more than 30 countries in the region (schooling profiles), and the procedures followed by more than 20 countries to organize lower secondary education, with very different economies of scale structures from one country to another.

21. Differences are due partly to the number of administrative personnel (whether 1 or 3 in a 120-student lower secondary school), and partly (1) to the degree of teacher polyvalence in different subjects and (2) to organization of curriculum content.

CHAPTER 7

Evaluating the Financing Gap

A key aim of the simulation exercise is to determine the amount of external aid that Sub-Saharan African (SSA) countries might require to attain their education goals. The simulation model includes all levels and types of education to provide a holistic, sectorwide picture, but the focus is on the post-primary system levels. The indicative benchmarks discussed in the foregoing chapters relate to the cost implications of countries' policy choices that affect the future size of enrollments by level and type of education and training and that influence service delivery arrangements. In this chapter, we consider the benchmarks for variables that determine the mobilization of domestic public spending, as well as the public-private division of responsibility for financing. The gap between aggregate costs and the resources that the country is able to mobilize provides a basis for estimating the resource gaps that external financing might contribute to fill.

BENCHMARKS AFFECTING VOLUME OF GOVERNMENT RESOURCES FOR EDUCATION

The relevant variables determining government resources allocated to education include the following:

- aggregate tax revenues as a percentage of gross domestic product (GDP)
- the education sector's share of overall government spending
- the share of primary education in government spending on education.

Because the benchmarks for these variables in the Education For All–Fast Track Initiative (EFA-FTI) indicative framework remain relevant, we retain them for the present exercise. In particular, for the first variable, the benchmarks are: 14, 16, or 18 percent of GDP, depending on the country's per capita GDP.[1] For the second variable, three benchmarks were used (shares of 20, 23, or 26 percent), each corresponding to a different simulation scenario. The model is structured such that if the share of education in overall government spending exceeds 20 percent (reflecting a high priority for education), all of the resources mobilized beyond this benchmark are channeled to the post-primary levels.

With regard to the third variable, the EFA-FTI benchmark of 50 percent was retained for the standard 6-year primary cycle; in countries where the cycle is longer than 6 years, the share is adjusted proportionally. Finally, in view of the whole sector perspective of this exercise, the model includes a variable to capture government spending on preschool education. The benchmark for this variable is set at the common reference level of 5 percent of total government spending on education. Taken together, the foregoing parameter values imply that at least 45 percent of overall government spending on education is effectively targeted in most countries to the post-primary levels.

BENCHMARKS FOR THE PUBLIC-PRIVATE DIVISION OF RESPONSIBILITY FOR EDUCATION

In all countries, there will always be some families that prefer and are able to afford private education for their children. In SSA, the share of privately financed enrollments averages about 10 percent at the primary level, 20 percent in the general stream of secondary education, 35 percent in the technical stream at the secondary level, and 17 percent in tertiary education.[2] As with many other aspects of education in SSA, there is great diversity across the 33 countries in our sample: in lower secondary schooling, for example, the share of enrollments in private schools ranges from 5 percent or less in Lesotho, Sierra Leone, and Zambia, to more than 45 percent in Rwanda and Uganda.

The diversity across countries makes it difficult to propose a common set of benchmarks for this simulation exercise. Two basic principles, equity and economic efficiency, were used to determine the choice of benchmarks. The first implies that primary schooling that is supposed to be universal should be free of charge to students because some parents cannot afford even minimal charges for schooling, so any cost would be sufficient to keep some children away, particularly girls and those from the poorest households. The second implies that individuals should share in the cost of their education if the benefits accrue mostly to the individuals themselves rather than to their communities. Because privately captured benefits generally rise with the level of education, there is a strong argument to favor the lower levels of education for public financing. The fact that social benefits from basic education are significant (for example, health gains, fertility behavior, and literacy) further strengthens this argument.

Based on these two principles and the cycle-specific considerations below, we chose the following benchmarks for the public-private division of responsibility for education in the simulation.

PRIMARY AND LOWER SECONDARY EDUCATION

For primary and lower secondary education, we retained the EFA-FTI indicative benchmark of 10 percent for the share of enrollments that are privately financed. This value simply leaves room for a small percentage in each population to exercise their choice for a different schooling service, one that is paid for privately. For lower secondary education, this assumption means that countries will move from the current share of some 20 percent private financing to 10 percent by 2020.

The current high share reflects the combined impact of several factors: the rise of private schooling to cope with the rapid increase in demand associated with the progress in universalizing primary education, the relative neglect of secondary education as countries prioritize the development of primary education, and the fact that secondary education is currently concentrated in urban areas where the market for private services is more developed. These conditions are unlikely to be sustained, however, as the coverage of lower secondary education is scaled up. Increasing shares of the school population will reside in rural areas and come from poorer strata of society; correspondingly, we expect the role of public sector provision to increase. Given that the goal is universal (or nearly universal) coverage by 2020, we have retained the same benchmark for private enrollment of 10 percent as the FTI benchmark for primary education.

UPPER SECONDARY EDUCATION

For the second cycle of general secondary education, the situation is structurally very different. Whereas a case can be made for progressively universalizing coverage in lower secondary education on equity and social grounds, the development of upper secondary education needs to be aligned more explicitly to preparing youth for work in the modern sector of the economy, either directly after this cycle or after further preparation at the tertiary level. Given the small size of the modern sector in most

SSA countries and its slow growth in the foreseeable future, an appropriate strategy for the development of upper secondary education is to put a greater emphasis on the quality of skills imparted to students who can benefit from the training than on the sheer number of students enrolled. Indeed, it is at this juncture of the education system that the issues of student flow regulation and the diversification of students' schooling careers come into sharp focus.

At this level in the system, substantial private financing is both more relevant as a mechanism for managing student flow and more justified by the usually high private returns to schooling. Public funding remains relevant, however, especially when targeted to support able students from modest backgrounds who might otherwise not be able to attend. Thus, for the simulations, we chose a benchmark of 40 percent by 2020 for the share of students that attend privately financed schools. Raising the share to this level from the current average of 20 percent would obviously require further thinking about the best way to make the transition toward a larger role for private financing at this level in the system (Walther 2005; World Bank, forthcoming).

SCHOOL-TO-WORK TRANSITION PROGRAMS

These programs are included in the structure of the simulation model as specific efforts that target young people who, at the end of primary or lower secondary education, discontinue their formal schooling. Such programs typically involve short-duration activities that seek to equip school leavers with life skills for the world of work, particularly in the informal economy where most of them can expect to earn their livelihoods. The programs are ideally implemented by the relevant professional bodies with government collaboration in the form of financing, rather than by direct involvement in service delivery. The programs serve two important functions: helping improve labor productivity in the informal sector and providing a socially acceptable way to relieve pressure on the upper levels of the formal schooling system. Because the clientele of these programs is likely to be predominantly from disadvantaged groups, for the purpose of the simulation exercise it was assumed that these programs would be funded in full by the government.

TECHNICAL AND VOCATIONAL EDUCATION AND TRAINING (TVET)

TVET in the simulation model implies formal courses of study that typically last two or three years in an institutional setting (either regular schools or specialized centers). They are in effect an alternative to the general stream in secondary education, and the curriculum may include work-based attachments to enhance student learning. The private sector plays an important role in providing this type of service, currently accounting for about 35 percent of enrollments, on average, among the 33 SSA countries in our sample. Experience suggests that private sector involvement, both in terms of financing and provision, helps ensure that training content is responsive to labor market needs, that training costs are kept in check, and that networks with prospective employers are developed to facilitate trainees' transition into working life. The simulation model benchmarks the share of private sector enrollment at 40 percent, with the expectation that the current role of the private sector would not only be maintained but indeed grow slightly stronger. Clearly, each country's strategy for attaining this benchmark will require additional discussion to define the most appropriate and effective strategy for implementation.

ACCESS TO TERTIARY EDUCATION

In higher education, many SSA countries have experienced sharp enrollment increases over the past decade with hardly any regulation of the student flow between the two cycles of secondary education and of access to tertiary education. Because aggregate public spending has not kept pace with the massive enrollment growth, conditions of service delivery have significantly deteriorated as stagnant budgets are stretched to cover more and more students. At the same time, large numbers of students have begun enrolling in private institutions, even though most of them have the option of entering virtually tuition-free public universities. Many of the private institutions are in fact relatively new, having sprung into existence to cater to strong student demand. It is estimated that the private sector currently accounts for at least 18 percent of students, on average, in the 33 SSA countries. For the same reasons discussed above for TVET, we envisaged a further enlargement of the private sector's role and therefore benchmarked its share of enrollment to rise to 40 percent by 2020. This increase is plausible in light of current developments in tertiary education and the success of many institutions in tapping private contributions as a source of income for their operations.

NOTES

1. The simulations use 14 percent for countries with GDP per capita less than $300, 16 percent when the GDP per capita is in the $300–600 range, and 18 percent for countries with GDP per capita above $600.

2. These shares are approximate and are likely to be underestimated, in part because the coverage of official statistics tends to be more complete for institutions in the public sector. Data are particularly sparse for private sector institutions offering technical education and training and post-secondary education.

8

Simulation Results

The simulation assumptions discussed in Chapters 5 to 7 regarding coverage, service delivery arrangements, and financing options, as well as the introduction of flexibility in setting country-specific benchmarks in light of per capita gross domestic product (GDP) levels and other conditions, have explicit implications for cost and financing gaps. These implications are presented below to illustrate potential combinations of strategic policy options for holistic development of education in Sub-Saharan Africa (SSA). This indispensable exercise is not a substitute for policy making but a tool that provides policy makers with critical information to evaluate the range of possibilities and consider the trade-offs that might be required to achieve their countries' education goals.

An important feature of the simulations is that, although they focus on the implications of policies in post-primary education, the scope of the model is in fact sectorwide, a feature that helps put the policies in proper context. We focus here on the aggregate results for all 33 SSA countries in the sample, which are a summation of country-specific computations (see the results reported by country in appendix E). Finally, to draw attention to the policy aspects of the exercise, although the simulations generate many results, only key results captured by the following variables are reported below in this chapter:

- the projected aggregate costs in 2020 to attain enrollment goals in primary, secondary, and tertiary education while diversifying the options for managing student flow
- the financing gap between the projected costs and what SSA countries might reasonably be able to mobilize from their own resources
- the implied dependency on external resources to attain the assumed goals given the policies in service delivery and domestic financing.

A RECAPITULATION OF THE KEY ASSUMPTIONS

A summary of key assumptions discussed earlier follows. The first set pertains to policies on education coverage. Five enrollment scenarios (ES) were explored, the first two distinctively different from the next three in terms of student flow management. In particular, the first two scenarios (ES-1 and ES-2) envision progress toward universal or nearly universal primary completion by 2020 and wide coverage in lower secondary cycle, followed by transition into tertiary education at current rates of transition from the previous cycle. In addition, the scenarios envision some diversification of educational options in the form of school-to-work life skills training and formal technical and vocational education and training. The other set of three enrollment scenarios (ES-3, ES-4, and ES-5) envision similar goals for coverage in primary and lower secondary education, but explicitly fix the size of enrollments in tertiary education (and hence of upper secondary education) in relation to expected employment opportunities in the formal sector of the economy. Because this sector is expected to remain relatively small in the foreseeable future, coverage at the upper levels of the system is expected also to remain limited. At the same time, the scenarios envision greater provision of school-to-work transition options to relieve the pressure on the formal education system, particularly at the upper secondary and tertiary levels. The last option considered is to combine the primary and lower secondary cycle into a basic cycle, which is relevant mainly because it reflects an organizational strategy to manage the cost of service delivery.

The second set of assumptions relates to policies about service delivery, which, as explained above, affect the cost of service delivery. In primary education, the same benchmarks as in the Education for All–Fast Track Initiative (EFA-FTI) framework were used for the pupil-teacher ratios, average teacher salaries, and spending on non-teacher inputs. The benchmarks on teacher salaries were adjusted upward for the poorest countries, as explained earlier. In secondary education, two sets of benchmarks were used, one to mirror relatively "generous" (that is, more expensive) service delivery conditions in terms of class size, teacher salaries, teaching loads, instruction time, and spending on non-teacher inputs), and the other to mirror relatively "spartan" (that is, more economical) conditions. The benchmarks for life skills training, technical and vocational education and training (TVET), and tertiary education are specified simply in terms of spending per student, and these are linked proportionally to the levels at the secondary level. In addition, for tertiary education, the model differentiates spending per student by field of study and computes average spending according to assumptions about the corresponding distribution of enrollments. It also recalls that the model computes the capital costs of classroom construction for primary and secondary schools.

Finally, the third set of assumptions relates to resource mobilization, both in terms of government allocation of public budgets and the distribution between publicly funded and privately funded enrollments. For resource mobilization, the benchmarks are the same as those in the EFA-FTI framework, while those for the public-private shares are chosen to reflect concerns about equity and efficiency. Thus, the values for the share of privately funded services are benchmarked at a modest level of about 10 percent for primary and lower secondary education and related school-to-work transition programs, but at the much higher rate of about 40 percent for study beyond lower secondary education.

SIMULATIONS OF AGGREGATE COSTS
AND FUNDING GAPS IN 2020

In the following, simulation results are shown for three different rates of growth in the per capita GDP between the base year and 2020. This variable affects the results in five ways. First, it influences the fiscal resources available for education. Second, because teachers' salaries are expressed as multiples of per capita GDP, the variable also affects the cost of service delivery. Third, for the poorest countries, the benchmarks for teachers' salaries have been adjusted to take into account the countries' current and projected levels of per capita GDP. Fourth, for some simulation scenarios, the enrollments in upper secondary and tertiary education are linked to the per capita GDP. Fifth—and perhaps most important— higher rates of per capita GDP growth imply higher absolute values in the level of spending per student and therefore larger aggregate costs expressed in absolute terms. For the purpose of this exercise, the assumed rates are: (1) 0 percent a year, which implies real GDP growing at the same rate as the population; (2) 2 percent a year, which implies that it would grow faster than the population by 2 percentage points; and (3) 4 percent a year, which corresponds more or less to the experience in SSA in the last decade, with real GDP growth averaging about 6.5 percent a year and population growth averaging 2.5 percent a year.

Table 8.1 summarizes the projected aggregate costs of service delivery in 2020, financing gaps, and dependency on external support under various policy scenarios, on the assumption that the real per capita GDP grows at a real rate of 2 percent a year. The results for higher and lower rates of growth are shown in Appendix D. For primary education, the financing

Table 8.1 **Aggregate Annual Public Spending on Education and Financing Gap in 2020 for 33 Low-Income SSA Countries**
2005 US$ billion unless otherwise indicated

Coverage	Policy scenario / Per-student spending at post-primary levels	Aggregate annual public education spending (recurrent and capital)	Annual recurrent financing gap in primary or basic education	Annual recurrent financing gap in post-primary education under 3 scenarios for domestic resource mobilization			Annual capital financing gap	Total financing gap as share of total public education spending (%)		
				Scenario 1	Scenario 2	Scenario 3		Scenario 1	Scenario 2	Scenario 3
ES-1	"Generous"	51.6	3.1	29.1	26.5	23.9	2.8	68	63	58
	"Spartan"	42.6		20.4	17.8	15.2	2.6	61	55	49
ES-2	"Generous"	44.8		22.7	20.0	17.4	2.5	63	57	51
	"Spartan"	37.9		16.0	13.4	10.8	2.3	56	49	42
ES-3	"Generous"	36.7		14.7	12.1	9.5	2.3	55	48	40
	"Spartan"	31.2		9.5	6.8	4.2	2.1	47	38	30
ES-4	"Generous"	31.5		9.7	7.2	5.0	2.1	47	39	31
	"Spartan"	27.2		5.6	3.2	1.1	1.9	39	29	20
ES-5	"Generous"	27.6	5.2	3.4	1.3	0.4	2.6	40	31	21
	"Spartan"	26.9		2.8	0.8	0.3	2.6	38	29	19

Notes: Rate of real growth of per capita GDP: 2 percent per year.
Enrollment scenarios: The five scenarios for coverage or enrollment are described on pages 16–18.
Resource mobilization scenarios: Scenarios 1–3 assume a budget allocation for education of 20%, 23%, and 26%, respectively, see also pages 43–44.
Shaded cells: Dependency on external financing 33% or less.

gap is, as expected, the same for different combinations of policies for the post-basic levels regarding coverage or enrollment (ES-1 to ES-4) and service delivery: $3.1 billion a year in 2020 for the 33 countries in the sample. With a structural change to attain universal coverage of nine years of basic education (ES-5), the gap would increase to $5.2 billion a year—an increase that would be compensated for by smaller gaps at the post-basic levels, as explained below.

At the post-primary levels, the funding gaps vary dramatically depending on the choice of policies. Gaps occur when the share of education in overall government spending is pegged at 20 percent (and the per capita GDP is growing at 2 percent a year). With the most expansive policy for coverage (ES-1) and the more generous assumptions for service delivery, the aggregate gap in recurrent funding in 2020 is estimated to be $29.1 billion a year for post-primary education and $3.1 billion a year for primary education (for a systemwide total of $32.2 billion a year). In addition, the 33 SSA countries would have a funding gap for capital investments in primary and secondary education of about $2.8 billion a year. Filling the gaps with external funds implies that these countries would depend on external funding sources for 68 percent of their expenditure on education. Both the absolute amounts and the rate of dependency are very high, possibly unrealistically so. More spartan choices in service delivery would reduce the post-primary recurrent funding gap significantly—to $20.4 billion a year—but its size and its implication for aid dependency (61 percent) remain challenging and very likely beyond thresholds that are feasible or even desirable.

With slightly less ambitious goals for the transition between primary and lower secondary education (that is, 80 percent instead of 100 percent), as captured by scenario ES-2, the recurrent funding gap in 2020 with generous policies for service delivery would amount to $22.7 billion a year for post-primary education and $3.1 billion a year for primary education, for a systemwide total of $25.8 billion a year, and the gap in capital spending on primary and secondary education would be $2.5 billion a year. Correspondingly, the level of aid dependency would fall only slightly to 63 percent (and with spartan service delivery policies to 56 percent). These figures are certainly lower than those for the scenario ES-1, but they are not fundamentally distinct in terms of the fiscal sustainability of the policies.

The next three enrollment scenarios—ES-3 to ES-5—mark a clear-cut departure from the previous two in that they reflect much more selective policies for coverage in upper secondary and tertiary education. Under scenario ES-3, the size of enrollments in tertiary education is benchmarked to tolerate a graduate unemployment rate of 25 percent, while the transition rate between primary and lower secondary education is retained at 80 percent. When service delivery policies are generous, the recurrent financing gap in 2020 would be $14.7 billion a year for post-primary education and $3.1 billion a year for primary education, and the gap in capital funding is projected at $2.3 billion a year. The corresponding dependency ratio would then be 55 percent. With spartan service delivery policies, the post-primary recurrent gap would fall to $9.5 billion a year and the dependency rate to 47 percent.

Under scenario ES-4, the assumed coverage in upper secondary and tertiary education is lowered to be consistent with a graduate unemployment rate of 20 percent instead of 25 percent, and the transition rate between primary and lower secondary education is reduced to 65 percent. The recurrent funding gap would then be $9.7 billion a year for post-primary education under generous service delivery policies and $5.6 billion a year under the spartan policies. The corresponding aid dependency rate would be 47 and 39 percent, respectively.

Finally, under scenario ES-5—which involves a structural change to provide 9 years of basic schooling and enrollments in upper secondary and tertiary education that are consistent with a graduate unemployment rate of 20 percent—the recurrent funding gap in post-basic education would be $3.4 billion a year with generous service delivery policies and $2.8 billion a year with spartan policies. As indicated above, this sharp fall compensates for the increased gap for basic education—$5.2 billion compared with $3.1 billion in the previous four enrollment scenarios. The gap in capital funding for basic and secondary education would be $2.6 billion a year, and the dependency on external support would fall to 40 percent with the generous service delivery policies and 38 percent with spartan policies.

Considering all the simulations obtained thus far, it is clear that with an education sector share of 20 percent in overall government recurrent spending and the assumed levels of private financing (which are relatively high, particularly in upper secondary and tertiary education), the implied funding gaps are massive under all ten combinations of policies in coverage and in service delivery. The prospects for mobilizing the required volume of external funding appear, at best, dim. If we accept as an upper limit that external funding exceeding 50 percent of what countries themselves spend would be untenable, then the maximum dependency ratio would be 33 percent.[1] By this somewhat normative but reasonable measure, none of the simulation scenarios considered thus far would meet the mark of acceptability. In view of this assessment, two further lines of exploration seem useful to consider in the simulation exercise: increase the budget allocation to the education sector and reduce the goal level of coverage or of the resource-intensity of service delivery.

Raising the budget share of education to 23 percent (ES-2) does indeed reduce the funding gap, as the relevant columns in table 8.1 show. However, accepting a cutoff dependency rate of 33 percent means that only the three cells shaded in grey in the table meet this criterion. They correspond to the following combinations of coverage and service delivery: (1) nine years of basic schooling (ES-5), with generous or spartan service delivery policies and (2) relatively tight controls on enrollments in upper secondary and tertiary education (ES-4) combined with spartan service delivery options. With a budget share of 26 percent, two additional policy combinations meet the criterion for acceptability: (1) ES-4 combined with generous service delivery policies and (2) slightly more ambitious goals for coverage in post-primary education (ES-3), but only with spartan choices for service delivery. Among the total of eight scenarios that imply a dependency rate no higher than 33 percent, all involve a model of discontinuity in student flow management in which enrollments in upper secondary and tertiary education are aligned to employment prospects for graduates. Even so, the dependency rate for these scenarios ranges from 19 percent to 31 percent—probably manageable but nonetheless still high.

The above figures assume that the per capita GDP would grow at an average of 2 percent a year between the base year and 2020. The results corresponding to per capita GDP growth rates of 0 and 4 percent a year are shown in appendix D. These results suggest that, in terms of dependency rates, using the threshold of 33 percent would confine the acceptable policy options to the same ones as those discussed above. This means that to achieve holistic development of education, it would be difficult for SSA countries to avoid the following:

- issues relating to budget priority for education
- proactive management of student flow, particularly in upper secondary and tertiary education, including options for diversifying the pathways for students to exit the system at lower levels into the workforce
- service delivery arrangements that would help keep a lid on costs.

However, the pace of growth in the per capita GDP affects the absolute size of the funding gaps (in international or national currency). As explained earlier, with a slower growth in per capita GDP than the 2 percent assumed thus far, these gaps would be smaller than the ones shown in the table 8.1; conversely, with a faster rate of growth, the gaps would be bigger. The funding gaps, while sizable under all scenarios, do vary significantly according to the projected rate of growth in the per capita GDP. Consider, for example, the scenario involving the ES-3 option for coverage, the spartan option for service delivery, and an allocation of 20 percent of government budget for education. The recurrent financing gap in 2020 would be $6.3 billion a year for post-primary education if the per capita GDP stagnated between the base year and 2020, $9.5 billion a year if it grew at 2 percent a year, and $16.4 billion a year if it grew at 4 percent over the period. Clearly, while sustained growth in the aid-receiving countries is clearly the ultimate objective, the simulation results confirm that, as countries grow richer, the cost of supporting their education programs, and hence the effort to mobilize external resources, will grow correspondingly higher.

DIVERSITY ACROSS THE SAMPLE OF 33 SSA COUNTRIES

The analysis above pertains to the aggregate picture for all 33 countries in our sample, based on the set of country-specific simulations shown in appendix E. This approach establishes general guidelines and overall orders of magnitude of financing gaps and dependency rates. It clearly needs to be supplemented with more detailed analysis in which the simulation assumptions are tailored to the specific conditions each country faces, especially because these conditions tend to vary widely across countries. Even without such second-stage analysis, the findings obtained thus far can help frame policy dialogue on the development of education in SSA.

Consider first the results for scenarios where the per capita GDP is growing at 2 percent a year. In this setting, only 9 of the 33 countries can envisage a dependency rate below 35 percent with policies in coverage corresponding to ES-1 and ES-2.[2] These countries are **Cameroon, Republic of Congo, The Gambia, Ghana, Guinea, Kenya, Lesotho, Mauritania, and Nigeria.** Five of these countries—Republic of Congo, The Gambia, Kenya, Lesotho, and Mauritania—are projected to have the lowest dependency ratios. The remaining four—Cameroon, Ghana, Guinea, and Nigeria—can maintain their dependency ratio below 35 percent while pursuing goals in coverage corresponding to ES-2 only if they also adopt spartan benchmarks for service delivery and allocate 26 percent of total government spending to the education sector.

For 8 of the 33 countries, none of the combinations of policies for coverage, for service delivery, and for domestic resource mobilization leads to a level of dependency on external financing that falls at or below

35 percent; this result holds true for all three rates of growth in the per capita GDP. These countries are Burundi, the Democratic Republic of Congo, Eritrea, Ethiopia, Guinea-Bissau, Malawi, Niger, and Sierra Leone. The results for Burkina Faso and Chad are very close to those of the previous eight countries. There is only one scenario leading to a level of dependency on external financing that falls at or below 35 percent; it corresponds to ES-5 combined with spartan options for service delivery and a 26 percent share of public spending allocated to education. For these ten countries, new simulation scenarios would be helpful to clarify the policy options that might warrant consideration aside from those included here. As the spartan options for service delivery are already quite basic, it may not be desirable, as far as ensuring minimum conditions in schools, to depart too far from the benchmarks used in this exercise. Accepting this argument leaves room for maneuvering only in terms of reducing the ambition of goals for coverage by 2020 or pushing back the horizon for achieving these goals or of raising the share of public spending allocated to the education sector beyond the 26 percent priority assumed in the most optimistic scenario. The prospect for such an increase poses very difficult intersectoral tradeoffs, however, since governments must also consider the needs of other sectors, such as health and agriculture.

For the remaining countries, the simulations present a more mixed picture. With a 4 percent per capita GDP growth between the base year and 2020, the rate of dependency on external funding would be manageable in **Benin, Côte d'Ivoire, Madagascar, Mozambique, Senegal, Sudan, Tanzania, Togo, and Zimbabwe** if the countries choose policies for coverage that correspond to ES-4 combined with spartan policies for service delivery and if they allocate a share of 23 percent of overall government spending to the sector. These policy options in Central African Republic, Mali, Rwanda, Uganda, and Zambia would also imply manageable dependency rates if the budget share of education rose to 26 percent.

While the foregoing results provide some insight into the nature of the policy challenges facing SSA countries, they are only a first step in policy development. In particular, some of the benchmarks, particularly those that define how educational services are organized, how much teachers are paid, and how much is spent on non-teaching inputs, cannot be detached from each country's historical, social, and political contexts. For example, implementing a move toward the benchmarks represented by spartan choices in service delivery may entail unrealistic decreases in the level of teacher salaries in some countries; and changing the teaching loads and instructional time for students may require reforms in curriculum and teacher training practices that may take time and effort to organize.[3]

In short, therefore, revisions and adjustments will be needed to make the simulation exercise pertinent for policy development in each of the 33 countries. The results, and more importantly, the simulation tool, represent a public good that is available to countries and to the development community, one that can be used as an aid for decision making and policy dialogue. While the tool can generate any number of policy scenarios, the challenge is to identify the combination of options that are sustainable in the medium term in terms of the requirements for national resources and external aid.

NOTES

1. As shown in the next chapter, a slightly higher cutoff of 35 percent has been used to evaluate the acceptability of simulation scenarios in individual countries; see also appendix E.

2. At present, external aid in SSA is, on average, about 16 percent of total public spending on education, ranging from less than 10 percent in such countries as the Republic of Congo, Lesotho, and Nigeria, to around 60 percent in Burundi, Mozambique, or Tanzania. Excluding Nigeria (a country with a large population and one that is not as dependent on aid as other SSA countries), the average for the remaining 32 other countries rises to 35 percent. It is indeed difficult to establish an undisputable benchmark to decide if this level of external funding is high or low and to evaluate whether it can (must) be increased, and if so, to what level. For the purpose of this report, we use a cutoff rate of 35 percent.

3. For example, a salary level representing about 5 times the GDP per capita is anticipated in lower secondary education while it represents about 9 times the GDP per capita in Togo and Mozambique at present.

CHAPTER 9

Conclusions

The development of post-primary education in Sub-Saharan Africa (SSA) is an emerging challenge in light of the progress that many of these countries have made in advancing the goal of universal primary school completion. For the purpose of this report, we constructed a sectorwide simulation model to characterize key policy scenarios and their implications regarding future enrollments and funding requirements. The model takes a sectorwide approach even though the focus is on policies at the post-primary levels, and it examines the prospects for funding under alternative scenarios for income growth. The results bring to light key issues for policy dialogue, not only within each country, but also between the 33 SSA countries included in this study and their development partners.

At heart, the issues pertain to fundamental questions:

How much domestic resources can countries themselves reasonably mobilize for education? How much foreign aid can the donor nations realistically contribute for the sector? What are acceptable levels of dependency on external aid in recipient and donor countries alike? What reforms in education sector policies—in terms of the pattern of coverage by level and type of education and of service delivery arrangements—will be required to put the education system on a sustainable path of development to meet national development goals? Although a technical study such as the present one cannot provide firm answers to these questions, its value lies in setting out the policy scenarios and evaluating their logistical and financial implications. In today's climate of global economic slowdown, such analysis has become especially pertinent.

Seven important conclusions emerge from the simulations, assuming that a dependency rate of 35 percent represents a threshold that few SSA countries and their donor partners would find acceptable to surpass. These conclusions are as follows:

- Policies that envision a significant expansion of coverage in the first cycle of secondary education combined with a model of continuity in student flow at subsequent levels generally fail the test of financial sustainability. Passing this test will typically require policies that regulate student flow more actively, so as to keep graduate unemployment rates at acceptable levels—a desirable goal in and of itself. Such policies include efforts to diversify curriculum options at the end of the first cycle of secondary education and also at the end of primary schooling as a temporary measure as long as lower secondary schooling is still not universal.

- Between the generous and spartan options for service delivery, the latter will probably be the more relevant one in most SSA countries. Although the practical feasibility of policies will depend on country context and implementation constraints, cost-conscious choices will often be unavoidable for countries to put the development of post-primary education on a financially sustainable path.

- To avoid an untenable dependency on external aid to finance educational development, SSA countries must typically exceed the 20 percent reference benchmark for the share of government spending allocated to the education sector. A minimum share of 23 percent seems relevant in most of the countries.

- The option of restructuring primary and lower secondary education into a single nine-year cycle of basic education is attractive in that aid dependency is lowest for this scenario, particularly when the policy is combined with spartan policies for service delivery. The advantage is not dramatic, however, because its main impact is to shift the distribution of the overall funding gap between basic education and post-basic education rather than reduce the absolute size of the gap itself. One drawback is that structural changes are disruptive and may cause misalignment between national and international qualification standards.

- While the 33 SSA countries in the sample share common goals and challenges, their specific circumstances in terms of initial conditions and political context are extremely varied. In light of the diversity across countries, the results of this simulation exercise are indeed indicative and must therefore be complemented by additional country-specific analysis. Such analysis can be prepared using either the tool developed for this study or other similar models.

- Faster rates of growth in the per capita incomes of SSA countries can be expected to facilitate the development of their education systems, in part by increasing the affordability of educational inputs that are purchased with domestic funds. Yet with income growth, the cost of services in absolute terms also rises. As a result, the absolute size of funding gaps also tends to increase even as the dependency rate falls.
- Finally, in all the policy scenarios considered in this paper, the development of post-primary development in the 33 SSA countries will require sizable volumes of external aid to fill funding gaps. The absolute amounts involved are as relevant as the level of aid dependency that they imply. Both issues belong on the agenda for policy dialogue within countries as well as between SSA countries and their development partners.

Relation Between Teacher Salaries and Country Income Level

1. As economies grow, average teacher salaries increase in absolute dollar terms, but tend to decline in relation to countries' gross domestic product (GDP) per capita (for an analysis of teacher salary trends in Sub-Saharan Africa (SSA) countries, see Mingat 2004). Based on a cross-country data set for Sub-Saharan Africa, the authors have estimated a statistical relation between primary teacher salaries, expressed in multiples of GDP per capita, and GDP per capita itself. The constant in the regression relation was subsequently adjusted so that it gives a salary of 3.5 times GDP per capita (indicative benchmark of the EFA-FTI) for a country with a GDP per capita of $350 (close to the average for SSA). The final relation is:

   Average primary teacher salary (in multiples of GDP per capita) = 4.2698 − 0.0022 ×; GDP per capita (in 2003 prices)

2. This relation is used in the simulation model to project teacher salaries for 2020 as a function of the level of income expected in that year. The relation is only used to calculate teacher salaries for countries with a GDP per capita less than $600, however. For countries with incomes above this benchmark, the simulations use a primary teacher salary of 3.0 times the GDP per capita for all (see table on page 64). As shown in the table, although salaries decline with higher per capita incomes, when measured relative to per capita GDP, they still grow when measured in constant U.S. dollars.

GDP per capita in 2020 (2003 prices)	100	150	200	350	500	≥ 600
Primary teacher salary in 2020:						
in multiples of GDP per capita	4.05	3.94	3.83	3.5	3.17	3.00
annual salary in US$ (2003 prices)	405	591	766	1,225	1,585	≥ 1,800

Note: Appendix E lists the teacher salaries used in the simulations for each of the 33 countries.

3. A similar adjustment is made for secondary school teacher salaries by raising (or lowering) the average salary by the same proportion above (below) the average benchmark as for primary education.

Basic Data for 33 SSA Countries

Table B.1 Quantitative Coverage of Education and Growth in Primary School Leavers

Country (base year)	Primary	Lower secondary		Upper secondary		TVET	Tertiary	Primary completers		
	Primary completion rate (%)	Transition rate P-S1 (%)	Gross intake rate (%)	Transition rate S1-S2 (%)	Gross intake rate (%)	Share of secondary enrollm. (%)	Students per 100 000 inhabitants	Number of students completing the cycle (thousands)		Ratio 2020/base year
								Base year	2020	
Benin (2004)	49.0	73.0	36.0	58.0	14.0	8.6	521	101.6	302.9	3.0
Burkina Faso (2004)	31.0	58.0	18.0	44.0	4.2	8.9	201	106.1	513.8	4.8
Burundi (2004)	33.1	52.2	17.3	44.3	3.5	9.7	228	65.5	318.1	4.9
Cameroon (2003)	57.6	56.3	32.4	64.5	18.7	23.4	494	231.3	438.6	1.9
Central African Rep. (2004)	30.0	56.4	16.8	78.9	5.4	6.4	233	30.8	116.4	3.8
Chad (2004)	37.8	72.0	26.0	80.0	10.0	1.6	117	91.0	384.5	4.2
Congo, Dem. Rep. (2005)	49.6	39.0	21.0	88.0	15.0	46.1	235	727.9	2,354.2	3.2
Congo, Rep. (2005)	72.0	79.2	57.1	37.1	16.2	24.3	337	74.4	165.5	2.2
Côte d'Ivoire (2000)	49.0	63.1	30.9	45.9	12.3	8.4	629	243.1	514.3	2.1
Eritrea (2005)	51.3	74.5	38.2	68.8	22.3	0.1	150	58.4	162.8	2.8
Ethiopia (2002)	53.0	78.7	42.0	77.5	14.5	1.6	138	1,050.4	2,640.5	2.5
Gambia, The (2001)	60.0	74.1	44.8	56.5	21.0	0.0	140	19.2	44.0	2.3
Ghana (2001)	66.0	98.8	65.0	40.0	22.4	1.6	354	340.3	589.1	1.7
Guinea (2005)	54.0	75.0	38.0	93.0	19.0	3.5	257	128.4	316.9	2.5
Guinea-Bissau (2002)	40.0	83.7	33.8	80.9	16.9	3.2	79	14.4	64.5	4.5
Kenya (2005)	70.0			47.0	30.0	16.8	279	584.6	1,177.0	2.0

Country									
Lesotho (2005)	69.4	76.0	51.0	84.0	24.0	1.4	380	33.4	38.4	1.1
Madagascar (2003)	37.0	65.0	28.5	52.4	7.7	10.3	205	168.2	623.2	3.7
Malawi (2002)	73.0	30.1	22.0	67.9	14.3	1.7	32	201.0	428.7	2.1
Mali (2004)	41.6	80.5	33.4	40.2	8.4	10.2	284	143.8	533.4	3.7
Mauritania (2004)	51.0	61.7	29.0	94.7	18.0	3.2	295	36.0	106.2	2.9
Mozambique (2001)	23.0	54.5	12.4	43.9	2.9	32.6	83	101.6	598.2	5.9
Niger (2002)	21.4	66.0	14.1	40.0	2.2	3.0	50	69.0	573.5	8.3
Nigeria (2005)	76.3	52.4	40.0	83.0	28.3	0.8	1,188	2,595.4	4,135.0	1.6
Rwanda (2003)	46.0	35.3	16.0	77.5	10.7	10.6	252	111.6	295.2	2.6
Senegal (2003)	49.0	54.0	27.0	62.9	11.0	6.6	496	143.0	357.0	2.5
Sierra Leone (2004)	55.0	63.0	35.0	39.2	10.0	15.4	269	68.1	183.0	2.7
Sudan (2003)	37.0	–	–	64.0	24.0	11.2	1,052	293.4	974.5	3.3
Tanzania (2002)	60.0	28.0	16.0	30.0	2.0	0.3	84	555.4	1,096.0	2.0
Togo (2005)	73.0	80.0	58.4	40.8	13.9	4.1	485	113.7	201.5	1.8
Uganda (2002)	51.0	44.6	22.6	40.0	7.1	7.1	292	344.4	1,312.7	3.8
Zambia (2005)	73.0	62.0	45.0	41.0	16.0	1.5	218	227.1	367.2	1.6
Zimbabwe (2003)	80.2	70.0	58.0	13.0	6.2	4.8	592	282.3	307.8	1.1
Avg. 33 countries	52.2	63.1	33.1	58.2	13.7	8.8	323	9,354.9	22,234.5	3.0*–2.4**

Source: Database compiled from Country Status Reports on Education, Public Expenditure Reviews, previous education sector simulation models, and UIS and EdStats databases. Population data used to calculate enrollment ratios are from United Nations.

* nonweighted average; ** average weighted by school-age population in the different countries. Dash = data not available.

Table B.2 Potential Growth in Lower Secondary Enrollment by Country

Country (base year)	Base year — Transition rate P-S1 (%)	Base year — Gross intake rate to lower secondary (%)	Base year — Lower secondary enrollm. (thousands)	2020 — Base year transition rate maintained — Gross intake rate to lower secondary (%)	2020 — Base year transition rate maintained — Lower secondary enrollm. (thousands)	2020 — Base year transition rate maintained — Ratio 2020/base year enrollm.	2020 — 100% transition — Enrollm. in lower secondary (thousands)	2020 — 100% transition — Ratio 2020/base year enrollm.
Benin (2004)	73.0	36.0	290.7	69.4	811.7	2.8	1,111.9	3.8
Burkina Faso (2004)	58.0	18.0	230.6	55.1	1,078.2	4.7	1,859.0	8.1
Burundi (2004)	52.2	17.3	121.8	49.6	550.9	4.5	1,055.4	8.7
Cameroon (2003)	56.3	32.4	559.8	52.3	944.8	1.7	1,717.7	3.1
Central African Rep. (2004)	56.4	16.8	57.8	53.6	251.0	4.3	445.1	7.7
Chad (2004)	72.0	26.0	211.3	68.4	974.1	4.6	1,352.8	6.4
Congo, Dem. Rep. (2005)	39.0	21.0	615.5	37.1	1,682.5	2.7	4,314.0	7.0
Congo, Rep. (2005)	79.2	57.1	259.0	75.2	466.6	1.8	589.1	2.3
Côte d'Ivoire (2000)	63.1	30.9	643.4	59.9	1,253.0	1.9	1,985.7	3.1
Eritrea (2005)	74.5	38.2	137.1	70.7	344.2	2.5	462.2	3.4
Ethiopia (2002)	78.7	42.0	2,579.2	74.8	7,782.5	3.0	9,888.8	3.8
Gambia, The (2001)	74.1	44.8	38.4	70.4	95.6	2.5	129.0	3.4
Ghana (2001)	98.8	65.0	941.3	93.9	1,703.9	1.8	1,724.6	1.8
Guinea (2005)	75.0	38.0	317.8	71.3	882.2	2.8	1,176.2	3.7
Guinea-Bissau (2002)	83.7	33.8	34.7	79.5	145.9	4.2	174.3	5.0
Kenya (2005)	—	—	—	—	—	—	—	—

Lesotho (2005)	76.0	51.0	65.4	72.2	87.5	1.3	115.2	1.8
Madagascar (2003)	65.0	28.5	422.2	61.8	1,533.1	3.6	2,358.5	5.6
Malawi (2002)	30.1	22.0	117.4	28.6	249.7	2.1	828.6	7.1
Mali (2004)	80.5	33.4	346.8	76.5	1,186.2	3.4	1,473.6	4.2
Mauritania (2004)	61.7	29.0	72.4	58.6	243.1	3.4	394.1	5.4
Mozambique (2001)	54.5	12.4	154.7	51.8	940.1	6.1	1,724.9	11.1
Niger (2002)	66.0	14.1	147.5	62.7	1,369.6	9.3	2,075.2	14.1
Nigeria (2005)	52.4	40.0	3,706.1	49.8	6,212.1	1.7	11,849.5	3.2
Rwanda (2003)	35.3	16.0	117.3	33.5	289.8	2.5	820.8	7.0
Senegal (2003)	54.0	27.0	279.2	51.3	735.1	2.6	1,361.3	4.9
Sierra Leone (2004)	63.0	35.0	125.1	59.9	320.9	2.6	509.4	4.1
Sudan (2003)	–	–	–	–	–	–	–	–
Tanzania (2002)	28.0	16.0	453.5	26.6	1,194.1	2.6	4,264.5	9.4
Togo (2005)	80.0	58.4	359.5	76.0	612.2	1.7	765.3	2.1
Uganda (2002)	44.6	22.6	507.7	42.4	2,003.8	3.9	4,492.9	8.8
Zambia (2005)	62.0	45.0	271.4	58.9	436.9	1.6	704.7	2.6
Zimbabwe (2003)	70.0	58.0	724.3	66.5	846.6	1.2	1,209.4	1.7
Average 33 countries	63.1	33.1	14,909.0	59.9	37,227.7	3.5*–2.5**	62,933.9	6.1*–4.2**

Source: Database compiled from Country Status Reports on Education, Public Expenditure Reviews, previous education sector simulation models, and UIS and EdStats databases. Population data used to calculate enrollment ratios are from United Nations.
* nonweighted average; ** average weighted by school-age population in the different countries. Dash = data not available.

Table B.3 School Organization in Lower Secondary Education, Circa 2005

Country (base year)	Average teacher salary (in multiples of GDP/capita)	Lower secondary				Per-student spending (in multiples of GDP/capita)
		Students per teacher (1)	Students per class (2)	Teachers per class (ratio (2)/(1))	Share of recurrent expenditure other than for teacher salaries (%)	
Benin (2004)	3.0	29.6	52.6	1.8	63.9	0.28
Burkina Faso (2004)	9.3	50.0	75.0	1.5	60.4	0.47
Burundi (2004)	9.3	20.5	42.4	2.1	29.1	0.64
Cameroon (2003)	6.5	31.1	40.3	1.3	34.3	0.32
Central African Rep. (2004)	4.8	56.7	78.0	1.4	44.1	0.15
Chad (2004)	4.4	40.6	59.7	1.5	44.4	0.19
Congo, Dem. Rep. (2005)	2.4	16.8	28.5	1.7	25.9	0.19
Congo, Rep. (2005)	2.3	63.8	86.0	1.3	70.2	0.12
Côte d'Ivoire (2000)	7.7	37.9	64.4	1.7	40.4	0.34
Eritrea (2005)	9.9	52.8	69.5	1.3	25.0	0.25
Ethiopia (2002)	8.1	48.3	67.8	1.4	18.6	0.21
Gambia, The (2001)	6.5	29.7	49.6	1.7	15.5	0.26
Ghana (2001)	3.9	18.5	18.5	1.0	29.7	0.30
Guinea (2005)	2.9	47.6	88.9	1.9	44.0	0.11
Guinea-Bissau (2002)	2.2	23.3	31.3	1.3	32.0	0.14
Kenya (2005)	—	—	—	—	—	—

Lesotho (2005)	9.0	26.7	50.0	1.9	27.0	0.46
Madagascar (2003)	4.3	27.2	44.0	1.6	41.7	0.27
Malawi (2002)	7.7	26.3	50.0	1.9	40.0	0.49
Mali (2004)	6.8	46.1	73.0	1.6	44.1	0.26
Mauritania (2004)	3.7	27.3	54.5	2.0	56.0	0.31
Mozambique (2001)	9.4	47.5	50.5	1.1	37.9	0.32
Niger (2002)	8.5	39.7	49.2	1.2	56.3	0.49
Nigeria (2005)	7.2	55.3	61.0	1.1	35.1	0.20
Rwanda (2003)	5.9	28.7	46.6	1.6	59.8	0.51
Senegal (2003)	6.2	39.0	60.7	1.6	27.5	0.22
Sierra Leone (2004)	5.9	29.4	49.0	1.7	30.1	0.29
Sudan (2003)	–	–	–	–	–	–
Tanzania (2002)	5.2	22.5	35.5	1.6	47.0	0.44
Togo (2005)	8.7	54.2	87.9	1.6	13.6	0.19
Uganda (2002)	7.4	6.8	15.2	2.2	25.1	1.45
Zambia (2005)	3.7	32.3	42.0	1.3	31.7	0.17
Zimbabwe (2003)	4.1	24.1	36.2	1.5	26.0	0.23
Average 33 countries	6.0	35.5	53.5	1.6	38.0	0.33

Source: Database compiled from Country Status Reports on Education, Public Expenditure Reviews, previous education sector simulation models, and UIS and EdStats databases. Dash = data not available.

Table B.4 School Organization in Upper Secondary Education, Circa 2005

Country (base year)	Average teacher salary (in multiples of GDP/capita)	Students per teacher (1)	Upper secondary Students per class (2)	Teachers per class (ratio (2)/(1))	Share of recurrent expenditure other than for teacher salaries (%)	Per-student spending (in multiples of GDP/capita)
Benin (2004)	5.2	20.4	46.0	2.3	63.9	0.71
Burkina Faso (2004)	13.0	39.0	52.0	1.3	48.0	0.64
Burundi (2004)	11.0	16.4	32.4	2.0	72.0	2.40
Cameroon (2003)	6.8	29.1	36.4	1.3	36.5	0.37
Central African Rep. (2004)	5.1	37.1	65.8	1.8	44.4	0.25
Chad (2004)	6.8	54.4	59.2	1.1	50.0	0.25
Congo, Dem. Rep. (2005)	2.4	16.8	28.5	1.7	25.9	0.19
Congo, Rep. (2005)	2.7	23.0	44.5	1.9	67.3	0.36
Côte d'Ivoire (2000)	8.9	23.5	39.9	1.7	40.4	0.63
Eritrea (2005)	11.8	45.0	70.3	1.6	25.0	0.35
Ethiopia (2002)	11.9	50.3	81.7	1.6	40.5	0.40
Gambia, The (2001)	6.5	17.3	34.8	2.0	20.6	0.47
Ghana (2001)	5.9	19.1	32.5	1.7	63.7	0.85
Guinea (2005)	2.9	52.3	95.0	1.8	41.0	0.09
Guinea-Bissau (2002)	2.2	23.3	31.3	1.3	32.0	0.14

Kenya (2005)	10.6	20.9	40.0	1.9	25.4	0.68
Lesotho (2005)	9.0	17.4	32.6	1.9	27.0	0.71
Madagascar (2003)	7.7	19.0	38.7	2.0	44.6	0.73
Malawi (2002)	7.7	26.3	50.0	1.9	40.0	0.49
Mali (2004)	8.3	23.1	39.6	1.7	69.3	1.17
Mauritania (2004)	4.8	20.3	42.8	2.1	44.7	0.42
Mozambique (2001)	23.8	26.4	45.7	1.7	34.7	1.38
Niger (2002)	10.2	13.0	33.2	2.6	49.9	1.57
Nigeria (2005)	7.2	44.9	52.9	1.2	35.8	0.25
Rwanda (2003)	6.4	21.8	40.1	1.8	54.0	0.63
Senegal (2003)	7.1	25.7	48.0	1.9	23.4	0.36
Sierra Leone (2004)	5.9	27.0	42.0	1.6	28.2	0.30
Sudan (2003)	3.4	26.7	53.5	2.0	28.6	0.18
Tanzania (2002)	5.2	22.5	35.5	1.6	47.0	0.44
Togo (2005)	9.0	33.3	62.4	1.9	15.9	0.32
Uganda (2002)	7.4	6.8	15.2	2.2	25.1	1.45
Zambia (2005)	4.7	25.3	45.0	1.8	26.7	0.25
Zimbabwe (2003)	4.1	24.1	41.0	1.7	26.0	0.23
Average 33 countries	7.4	27.1	45.7	1.8	39.9	0.60

Source: Database compiled from Country Status Reports on Education, Public Expenditure Reviews, previous education sector simulation models, and UIS and EdStats databases.

Table B.5　School Organization in Primary and Tertiary Education, Circa 2005

Country (base year)	Primary				Tertiary
	Average teacher salary (in multiples of GDP/capita)	Students per teacher	Share of recurrent expenditure other than for teacher salaries (%)	Per-student spending (in multiples of GDP/capita)	Per-student spending (in multiples of GDP/capita)
Benin (2004)	4.2	52.0	39.5	0.11	1.6
Burkina Faso (2004)	6.4	52.8	33.8	0.18	2.4
Burundi (2004)	6.8	51.7	13.2	0.15	8.3
Cameroon (2003)	3.9	63.7	30.8	0.07	0.8
Central African Rep. (2004)	7.0	91.6	34.3	0.07	2.4
Chad (2004)	5.4	70.3	37.8	0.05	3.3
Congo, Dem. Rep. (2005)	2.2	37.7	26.0	0.05	2.2
Congo, Rep. (2005)	1.8	75.7	68.0	0.05	2.0
Côte d'Ivoire (2000)	4.8	42.6	25.0	0.15	1.1
Eritrea (2005)	3.9	43.7	25.3	0.12	4.3
Ethiopia (2002)	6.8	73.9	16.0	0.11	11.2
Gambia, The (2001)	4.5	36.5	21.8	0.16	3.8
Ghana (2001)	3.9	32.9	28.1	0.16	3.7
Guinea (2005)	1.7	51.3	44.2	0.06	1.5
Guinea-Bissau (2002)	1.9	37.5	31.0	0.07	1.2

Kenya (2005)	5.3	39.7	17.9	0.16	2.6
Lesotho (2005)	4.4	46.0	46.6	0.18	7.9
Madagascar (2003)	4.4	57.7	42.8	0.09	2.1
Malawi (2002)	4.2	58.4	15.0	0.08	14.9
Mali (2004)	6.0	63.5	37.8	0.11	1.9
Mauritania (2004)	3.3	44.2	31.8	0.11	0.9
Mozambique (2001)	3.9	55.0	22.6	0.09	6.6
Niger (2002)	5.5	42.9	35.0	0.20	5.7
Nigeria (2005)	4.9	51.7	34.2	0.14	1.1
Rwanda (2003)	3.9	60.3	22.2	0.08	7.9
Senegal (2003)	4.6	50.8	37.6	0.15	2.8
Sierra Leone (2004)	4.2	61.0	30.9	0.09	3.4
Sudan (2003)	2.2	36.0	22.5	0.08	1.1
Tanzania (2002)	3.8	46.2	34.0	0.12	5.3
Togo (2005)	6.2	33.6	12.8	0.10	1.3
Uganda (2002)	3.2	56.1	31.7	0.08	1.9
Zambia (2005)	3.1	57.2	28.2	0.07	2.9
Zimbabwe (2003)	4.1	39.0	21.0	0.13	2.3
Average 33 countries	4.3	51.9	30.3	0.11	3.7

Source: Database compiled from Country Status Reports on Education, Public Expenditure Reviews, previous education sector simulation models, and UIS and EdStats databases.

Table B.6 Population Growth Rates Used in Simulations

Country (base year)	Average annual growth in primary school-age population (age 6–11)					Average annual growth rate in total population 2000–2020
	2000–2005	2005–2010	2010–2015	2015–2020	Average 2000–2020	
Benin (2004)	2.6	2.6	2.6	2.1	2.5	2.9
Burkina Faso (2004)	2.6	2.6	2.9	2.6	2.7	3.0
Burundi (2004)	0.8	2.4	4.9	4.6	3.2	3.2
Cameroon (2003)	0.9	0.8	0.6	0.3	0.7	1.6
Central African Rep. (2004)	1.5	0.8	0.8	1.0	1.0	1.4
Chad (2004)	3.5	2.7	3.2	3.3	3.2	3.0
Congo, Dem. Rep. (2005)	2.6	3.4	3.6	3.0	3.2	3.0
Congo, Rep. (2005)	3.4	3.3	3.3	3.2	3.3	3.1
Côte d'Ivoire (2000)	0.9	0.9	0.9	0.8	0.9	1.7
Eritrea (2005)	4.3	3.1	2.3	1.6	2.8	3.1
Ethiopia (2002)	2.1	1.7	1.7	1.6	1.8	2.3
Gambia, The (2001)	2.7	2.2	1.1	0.5	1.6	2.3
Ghana (2001)	0.8	1.0	0.9	0.6	0.8	1.9
Guinea (2005)	2.0	2.0	2.3	2.0	2.1	2.3
Guinea-Bissau (2002)	3.5	3.2	3.4	3.0	3.3	3.0
Kenya (2005)	1.0	2.8	3.4	1.9	2.3	2.4
Lesotho (2005)	-1.4	-1.1	-0.5	0.0	-0.8	-0.2
Madagascar (2003)	3.1	2.1	1.5	1.4	2.0	2.5

Malawi (2002)	3.9	1.9	1.3	1.7	2.2	2.2
Mali (2004)	3.3	2.8	2.7	2.6	2.8	3.0
Mauritania (2004)	3.0	3.1	2.4	1.5	2.5	2.7
Mozambique (2001)	2.2	1.5	1.2	1.0	1.4	1.8
Niger (2002)	4.1	3.6	2.8	2.8	3.3	3.3
Nigeria (2005)	1.8	1.6	1.4	1.1	1.5	2.0
Rwanda (2003)	0.1	1.7	2.3	1.8	1.5	2.2
Senegal (2003)	1.4	1.6	1.4	0.9	1.3	2.2
Sierra Leone (2004)	4.2	2.4	2.5	2.2	2.8	2.7
Sudan (2003)	1.6	1.6	0.8	0.3	1.1	1.9
Tanzania (2002)	1.4	1.2	0.8	0.6	1.0	1.8
Togo (2005)	2.3	2.2	1.7	1.1	1.8	2.5
Uganda (2002)	3.4	3.7	4.3	4.1	3.9	3.7
Zambia (2005)	1.4	1.3	1.4	1.5	1.4	1.7
Zimbabwe (2003)	-0.9	-0.9	0.1	0.5	-0.3	0.6

Source: United Nations population projections, 2006 revision.

APPENDIX C

Schematic Summary
of Scenarios

Table C.1 Options in Simulation Model for Coverage, Level of Per-Student Spending, and Share of Private Financing in 2020

Coverage options	Primary		Lower secondary			Upper secondary			Tertiary		
	Duration (years)	Primary completion rate (%)	Transition rate P-S1 (%)	Share enrolled in TVET (%)	Share of primary school leavers not enrolled in lower sec., who enter school-to-work transition program	Upper sec. enrollm. in multiples of tertiary enrollm.	Share enrolled in TVET (%)	Share of lower sec. school leavers not enrolled in upper sec., who enter school-to-work transition program	Unemployment cutoff rate used to determine tertiary enrollment	Share enrolled in sciences (%)	Share enrolled in professional (%)
ES-1		95	100	10			15	50			
ES-2		95	80	15	50		15	50			
ES-3		95	80	15	50	2.5	25	100	25	15	25
ES-4		95	65	20	50	2.5	15	50	20	15	25
ES-5	9	95/80[a]				2.5	15	50	20	15	25

		Lower secondary			Upper secondary			Tertiary		
	Primary	General lower sec.	TVET lower sec.	School-to-work transition program	General upper sec.	TVET upper sec.	School-to-work transition program	Humanities & social sciences	Sciences	Professional
Level of per-student spending in % of per capita GDP[b]										
"Generous"		35.4	90	50	60.9	140	100	150	240	290
"Spartan"	13/15[c]	17.7	90	50	32.2	140	100	150	240	290
Share of enrollment in privately-financed schools	10	10	10	0	40	40	0	40	40	40

Note: Shaded cell indicates no change in the indicator between the base year and 2020.

a. The first number indicates the completion rate of the first 6 years (or whatever the duration of the primary cycle) and the second the completion rate of the 9-year cycle.

b. This parameter describes the "basic" level of per-student spending before any adjustment for level of wealth, geographic dimension, or stimulation of demand. Appendix E provides the country-specific values for per-student spending used in the simulations.

c. The first number indicates the per-student spending for the 6-year primary cycle (or whatever the duration of the primary cycle) and the second number reflects the per-student spending for the 9-year cycle.

	Unit cost of classroom construction (2005 US$)
Primary	12,000
Lower secondary	16,000
Upper secondary	16,000

APPENDIX D

Aggregate Simulation Results

Table D.1 Student Enrollment by Level of Education in 2020 for 33 Low-Income SSA Countries, Assuming 0% Real Growth of GDP per Capita per Year
US$ million

Year	Coverage scenario	Transition rate P-S1	Transition beyond S1	Primary	Lower secondary			Upper secondary			Tertiary
					General	TVET	School-to-work transition program	General	TVET	School-to-work transition program	
Base year		63%	–	100.4	13.8	n/a	n/a	7.2	n/a	n/a	3.0
2020	ES-1	100%	"Continuity"	161.0	56.6	5.7	0.0	25.8	3.5	2.7	13.8
	ES-2	80%			42.8	6.9	2.0	20.4	2.7	2.1	10.8
	ES-3	80%	"Discontinuity"		42.8	6.9	2.0	4.9	1.3	9.9	2.6
	ES-4	65%			32.7	7.5	3.4	4.7	0.7	3.9	2.2
	ES-5	9 years of primary	"Discontinuity"	211.6		0.0	0.0	5.1	0.7	7.7	2.2

Note: Rate of real growth of per capita GDP: 0% per year.
Appendix E provides the corresponding simulation results for each of the 33 countries.

Table D.2 Student Enrollment by Level of Education in 2020 for 33 Low-Income SSA Countries, Assuming 4% Real Growth of GDP per Capita per Year
US$ million

Year	Coverage scenario	Transition rate P-S1	Transition beyond S1	Primary	Lower secondary			Upper secondary			
					General	TVET	School-to-work transition program	General	TVET	School-to-work transition program	Tertiary
Base year		63%	–	100.4	13.8	n/a	n/a	7.2	n/a	n/a	3.0
2020	ES-1	100%	"Continuity"	161.0	56.6	5.7	0.0	25.8	3.5	2.7	13.8
	ES-2	80%			42.8	6.9	2.0	20.4	2.7	2.1	10.8
	ES-3	80%	"Discontinuity"		42.8	6.9	2.0	8.1	2.2	8.4	4.4
	ES-4	65%			32.7	7.5	3.4	7.1	1.0	3.5	3.3
	ES-5	9 years of primary	"Discontinuity"	211.6		0.0	0.0	7.8	1.0	7.2	3.3

Note: Rate of real growth of per capita GDP: 4% per year.
Appendix E provides the corresponding simulation results for each of the 33 countries.

Table D.3 Aggregate Annual Public Spending on Education and Financing Gap in 2020 for 33 SSA Countries, Assuming 0% Real Growth of GDP per Capita per Year

2005 US$ billion

Policy scenario		Aggregate annual public education spending (recurrent and capital)	Annual recurrent financing gap in primary or basic education	Annual recurrent financing gap in post-primary education under 3 scenarios for domestic resource mobilization			Annual capital financing gap	Total financing gap as share of total public education spending (%)		
Coverage	Per-student spending at post-primary levels			Scenario 1	Scenario 2	Scenario 3		Scenario 1	Scenario 2	Scenario 3
ES-1	"Generous"	38.8	2.6	21.3	19.4	17.5	2.8	69	64	59
	"Spartan"	32.1		14.9	13.0	11.1	2.6	63	57	51
ES-2	"Generous"	33.7		16.6	14.7	12.8	2.5	64	59	53
	"Spartan"	28.6		11.7	9.8	7.9	2.3	58	51	45
ES-3	"Generous"	26.9		10.0	8.1	6.2	2.3	55	48	41
	"Spartan"	23.0		6.3	4.4	2.5	2.1	48	40	31
ES-4	"Generous"	23.4		6.7	4.9	3.2	2.1	49	40	32
	"Spartan"	20.3		3.7	2.0	0.7	1.9	41	31	22
ES-5	"Generous"	21.2	4.8	2.0	0.5	0.2	2.6	43	34	25
	"Spartan"	20.7		1.6	0.3	0.1	2.6	42	33	24

Notes: Rate of real growth of per capita GDP: 0% per year.

Enrollment scenarios: The five scenarios for coverage or enrollment are described on pages 16–18.

Resource mobilization scenarios: Scenarios 1–3 assume a budget allocation for education of 20%, 23%, and 26%, respectively, see also pages 43–44.

Shaded cells: Dependency on external financing 33% or less.

Appendix E provides the corresponding simulation results for each of the 33 countries.

Table D.4 Aggregate Annual Public Spending on Education and Financing Gap in 2020 for 33 SSA Countries, Assuming 4% Real Growth of GDP per Capita per Year

2005 US$ billion

Policy scenario		Aggregate annual public education spending (recurrent and capital)	Annual recurrent financing gap in primary or basic education	Annual recurrent financing gap in post-primary education under 3 scenarios for domestic resource mobilization			Annual capital financing gap	Total financing gap as share of total public education spending (%)		
Coverage	Per-student spending at post-primary levels			Scenario 1	Scenario 2	Scenario 3		Scenario 1	Scenario 2	Scenario 3
ES-1	"Generous"	69.1	3.9	39.6	36.0	32.4	2.8	67	62	57
	"Spartan"	57.1		27.9	24.3	20.7	2.6	60	54	48
ES-2	"Generous"	60.0		30.8	27.2	23.6	2.5	62	56	50
	"Spartan"	50.8		21.9	18.3	14.7	2.3	55	48	41
ES-3	"Generous"	53.0		24.0	20.4	16.8	2.3	57	50	43
	"Spartan"	45.1		16.4	12.8	9.2	2.1	50	42	34
ES-4	"Generous"	44.5		15.8	12.2	9.1	2.1	49	41	33
	"Spartan"	38.4		9.8	6.4	3.3	2.0	41	31	22
ES-5	"Generous"	39.4	6.7	7.4	4.4	2.2	2.6	42	33	24
	"Spartan"	37.9		6.0	3.1	1.6	2.6	40	30	21

Notes: Rate of real growth of per capita GDP: 4% per year.

Enrollment scenarios: The five scenarios for coverage or enrollment are described on pages 16–18.

Resource mobilization scenarios: Scenarios 1–3 assume a budget allocation for education of 20%, 23%, and 26%, respectively; see also pages 43–44.

Shaded cells: Dependency on external financing 33% or less.

Appendix E provides the corresponding simulation results for each of the 33 countries.

APPENDIX E

Simulation Results by Country

BENIN

BENIN: Enrollments Under Different Policy Scenarios, Base Year and 2020

			Lower secondary			Upper secondary			
		Primary	General	TVET	School-to-work transition program	General	TVET	School-to-work transition program	Tertiary
	2004	1,462,170	297,964	n/a	n/a	62,569	n/a	n/a	41,282
2020	ES-1	2,128,871	1,000,736	84,499	0	309,675	53,172	33,634	236,395
	ES-2	2,128,871	756,111	101,399	29,556	233,977	40,174	25,412	178,609
	ES-3	2,128,871	756,111	101,399	29,556	75,414	24,458	110,735	41,375
	ES-4	2,128,871	578,203	109,849	51,724	70,233	12,059	41,357	33,999
	ES-5	2,854,576				94,984	12,403	100,940	33,999

Note: Rate of real growth of per capita GDP: 2% per year.

BENIN: GER and Other Parameters Under Different Policy Scenarios, Base Year and 2020

			Lower secondary GER (%)			Upper secondary GER (%)			Higher education GER (%) and other indicators		
		Primary GER (%)	General	TVET	School-to-work transition program	General	TVET	School-to-work transition program	GER (%)	Students/ 100,000	Unemployment (simulated) (%)
	2004	109.6	38.4	n/a	n/a	11.9	n/a	n/a	6.7	505	n/a
2020	ES-1	108.3	85.5	9.5	0.0	38.8	6.7	12.0	24.5	1,859	51
	ES-2	108.3	64.6	11.4	9.5	29.3	5.0	9.0	18.5	1,405	48
	ES-3	108.3	64.6	11.4	9.5	9.5	3.1	39.4	4.3	325	25
	ES-4	108.3	49.4	12.4	16.6	8.8	1.5	14.7	3.5	267	20
	ES-5	100.0				8.8	1.5	35.0	3.5	267	20

Note: Rate of real growth of per capita GDP: 2% per year.

BENIN: Teacher Salaries and Per-Student Spending by Level of Education, Base Year and 2020

		Lower secondary			Upper secondary			Higher education			
	Primary	General	TVET	School-to-work transition program	General	TVET	School-to-work transition program	Humanities & social sciences	Sciences	Professional	All
Teacher salaries in multiples of per capita GDP[a]											
2004	4.2	3.0			5.2						
2020 "Generous"[b]	3.0/3.2[b]	4.6			5.9						
"Spartan"	4.2	4.2			5.1						
Level of per-student spending in % of per capita GDP[a]											
2004	13	28	113	110	71	113	33	119	136	180	137
2020 "Generous"[b]	13/15[b]	37	90	50	55	140	100	151	242	291	200
"Spartan"	18	18	90	50	29	140	100	151	242	291	200

Note: Rate of real growth of per capita GDP: 2% per year.
a. After adjustment for wealth, geographic dimension, and/or stimulation of demand.
b. The first number pertains to the 6-year primary cycle (or whatever the duration of the primary cycle) and the second number to the 9-year primary cycle in ES-5.

BENIN: Estimated Annual Public Spending on Education and Financing Gap in 2020

2005 US$ million unless otherwise indicated

Policy scenario		Aggregate annual public education spending (recurrent and capital)	Annual recurrent financing gap in **primary or basic education**	Annual recurrent financing gap in **post-primary education** under 3 scenarios for domestic resource mobilization			Annual capital financing gap	Total financing gap as share of total public education spending (%)		
Coverage	Per-student spending at post-primary levels			Scenario 1	Scenario 2	Scenario 3		Scenario 1	Scenario 2	Scenario 3
ES-1	"Generous"	788		444	401	359	43	66	61	55
	"Spartan"	635		296	253	211	38	58	51	44
ES-2	"Generous"	673		336	293	251	37	60	54	47
	"Spartan"	558		224	181	139	33	52	44	37
ES-3	"Generous"	570		235	193	150	34	53	45	38
	"Spartan"	472		141	98	56	31	43	34	25
ES-4	"Generous"	490		159	116	74	30	45	36	28
	"Spartan"	413	32	85	43	0	28	35	25	14
ES-5	"Generous"	405		48	5	-37	36	34	23	13
	"Spartan"	394	52	38	-5	-47	36	32	21	10

Notes: Rate of real growth of per capita GDP: 2% per year.
Enrollment scenarios: The five scenarios for coverage or enrollment are described on pages 16–18.
Resource mobilization scenarios: Scenarios 1–3 assume a budget allocation for education of 20%, 23%, and 26%, respectively; see also pages 43–44.
Shaded cells: Dependency on external financing 35% or less.

BURKINA FASO

BURKINA FASO: Enrollments Under Different Policy Scenarios, Base Year and 2020

		Primary	Lower secondary			Upper secondary			Tertiary
			General	TVET	School-to-work transition program	General	TVET	School-to-work transition program	
2004		1,120,726	217,104	n/a	n/a	41,581	n/a	n/a	24,975
2020	ES-1	3,654,662	1,673,066	141,539	0	511,464	87,819	55,891	406,654
	ES-2	3,654,662	1,264,094	169,846	49,943	386,439	66,352	42,228	307,250
	ES-3	3,654,662	1,264,094	169,846	49,943	107,953	35,012	191,647	59,590
	ES-4	3,654,662	966,660	184,000	87,401	102,974	17,681	71,366	50,154
	ES-5	4,863,415				139,487	18,240	171,073	50,154

Note: Rate of real growth of per capita GDP: 2% per year.

BURKINA FASO: GER and Other Parameters Under Different Policy Scenarios, Base Year and 2020

		Primary GER (%)	Lower secondary GER (%)			Upper secondary GER (%)			Higher education GER (%) and other indicators		
			General	TVET	School-to-work transition program	General	TVET	School-to-work transition program	GER (%)	Students/ 100,000	Unemployment (simulated) (%)
2004		50.7	17.2	n/a	n/a	5.0	n/a	n/a	2.6	195	n/a
2020	ES-1	108.3	85.5	9.5	0.0	38.8	6.7	12.0	25.8	2,003	55
	ES-2	108.3	64.6	11.4	9.5	29.3	5.0	9.0	19.5	1,513	51
	ES-3	108.3	64.6	11.4	9.5	8.2	2.7	41.0	3.8	293	25
	ES-4	108.3	49.4	12.4	16.6	7.8	1.3	15.3	3.2	247	20
	ES-5	100.0				7.8	1.3	35.5	3.2	247	20

Note: Rate of real growth of per capita GDP: 2% per year.

BURKINA FASO: Teacher Salaries and Per-Student Spending by Level of Education, Base Year and 2020

	Primary	Lower secondary			Upper secondary			Higher education			
		General	TVET	School-to-work transition program	General	TVET	School-to-work transition program	Humanities & social sciences	Sciences	Professional	All
Teacher salaries in multiples of per capita GDP[a]											
2004	6.4	9.3			13.0						
2020 "Generous"	3.0/3.2[b]	4.6			6.0						
"Spartan"		4.2			5.1						
Level of per-student spending in % of per capita GDP[a]											
2004	18	47	90	110	64	90	33	182	207	275	209
2020 "Generous"	14/16[b]	41	90	50	62	140	100	196	314	379	259
"Spartan"		20	90	50	32	140	100	196	314	379	259

Note: Rate of real growth of per capita GDP: 2% per year.
a. After adjustment for wealth, geographic dimension, and/or stimulation of demand.
b. The first number pertains to the 6-year primary cycle (or whatever the duration of the primary cycle) and the second number to the 9-year primary cycle in ES-5.

BURKINA FASO: Estimated Annual Public Spending on Education and Financing Gap in 2020

2005 US$ million unless otherwise indicated

Policy scenario		Aggregate annual public education spending (recurrent and capital)	Annual recurrent financing gap in **primary or basic education**	Annual recurrent financing gap in **post-primary education** under 3 scenarios for domestic resource mobilization			Annual capital financing gap	Total financing gap as share of total public education spending (%)		
Coverage	Per-student spending at post-primary levels			Scenario 1	Scenario 2	Scenario 3		Scenario 1	Scenario 2	Scenario 3
ES-1	"Generous"	1,317		812	764	716	92	77	73	70
	"Spartan"	1,081		585	537	488	84	72	67	63
ES-2	"Generous"	1,115		621	573	525	81	73	68	64
	"Spartan"	937		449	401	353	75	67	62	57
ES-3	"Generous"	868		378	330	282	77	65	59	54
	"Spartan"	719		235	187	139	71	58	51	44
ES-4	"Generous"	753		270	222	173	70	59	53	47
	"Spartan"	636	108	158	110	62	65	52	45	37
ES-5	"Generous"	625		82	33	−15	75	51	43	36
	"Spartan"	610	163	68	19	−29	74	50	42	34

Notes: Rate of real growth of per capita GDP: 2% per year.

Enrollment scenarios: The five scenarios for coverage or enrollment are described on pages 16–18.

Resource mobilization scenarios: Scenarios 1–3 assume a budget allocation for education of 20%, 23%, and 26%, respectively; see also pages 43–44.

Shaded cells: Dependency on external financing 35% or less.

BURUNDI

BURUNDI: Enrollments Under Different Policy Scenarios, Base Year and 2020

			Lower secondary			Upper secondary			
		Primary	General	TVET	School-to-work transition program	General	TVET	School-to-work transition program	Tertiary
2004		983,984	126,110	3,330	n/a	24,073	n/a	n/a	24,975
2020	ES-1	2,321,824	949,892	81,266	0	268,965	46,182	30,589	216,360
	ES-2	2,321,824	717,696	97,519	30,099	203,218	34,893	23,112	163,472
	ES-3	2,321,824	717,696	97,519	30,099	48,271	15,656	108,959	27,732
	ES-4	2,321,824	548,826	105,646	52,673	49,352	8,474	40,073	25,017
	ES-5	2,998,656				67,565	8,911	96,924	25,017

Note: Rate of real growth of per capita GDP: 2% per year.

BURUNDI: GER and Other Parameters Under Different Policy Scenarios, Base Year and 2020

			Lower secondary GER (%)			Upper secondary GER (%)			Higher education GER (%) and other indicators		
		Primary GER (%)	General	TVET	School-to-work transition program	General	TVET	School-to-work transition program	GER (%)	Students/ 100,000	Unemployment (simulated) (%)
2004		79.9	16.7	0.6	n/a	4.7	n/a	n/a	2.7	221	n/a
2020	ES-1	108.3	85.5	9.5	0.0	38.8	6.7	12.0	26.7	1,764	61
	ES-2	108.3	64.6	11.4	9.5	29.3	5.0	9.0	20.2	1,333	58
	ES-3	108.3	64.6	11.4	9.5	7.0	2.3	42.6	3.4	226	25
	ES-4	108.3	49.4	12.4	16.6	7.1	1.2	15.7	3.1	204	20
	ES-5	100.0				7.1	1.2	35.9	3.1	204	20

Note: Rate of real growth of per capita GDP: 2% per year.

BURUNDI: Teacher Salaries and Per-Student Spending by Level of Education, Base Year and 2020

	Primary	Lower secondary			Upper secondary			Higher education			
		General	TVET	School-to-work transition program	General	TVET	School-to-work transition program	Humanities & social sciences	Sciences	Professional	All
Teacher salaries in multiples of per capita GDP[a]											
2004	6.8	9.3			11.0						
2020 "Generous"	4.0/4.2[b]	6.1			7.8						
"Spartan"		5.6			6.8						
Level of per-student spending in % of per capita GDP[a]											
2004	15	64	220	110	240	220	33	615	702	932	707
2020 "Generous"	23/26[b]	69	90	50	109	140	100	331	530	640	438
"Spartan"	33	33	90	50	54	140	100	331	530	640	438

Note: Rate of real growth of per capita GDP: 2% per year.
a. After adjustment for wealth, geographic dimension, and/or stimulation of demand.
b. The first number pertains to the 6-year primary cycle (or whatever the duration of the primary cycle) and the second number to the 9-year primary cycle in ES-5.

BURUNDI: Estimated Annual Public Spending on Education and Financing Gap in 2020

2005 US$ million unless otherwise indicated

Coverage	Per-student spending at post-primary levels	Aggregate annual public education spending (recurrent and capital)	Annual recurrent financing gap in **primary or basic education**	Annual recurrent financing gap in **post-primary education** under 3 scenarios for domestic resource mobilization			Annual capital financing gap	Total financing gap as share of total public education spending (%)		
				Scenario 1	Scenario 2	Scenario 3		Scenario 1	Scenario 2	Scenario 3
ES-1	"Generous"	293		163	156	150	50	86	84	81
	"Spartan"	238		113	106	100	45	83	80	77
ES-2	"Generous"	247		124	117	111	43	83	81	78
	"Spartan"	206		79	73	40	80	77	73	
ES-3	"Generous"	195		73	67	60	41	79	75	72
	"Spartan"	160		35	29	38	74	70	66	
ES-4	"Generous"	172		55	48	42	37	76	72	68
	"Spartan"	145	39	30	24	17	35	71	67	62
ES-5	"Generous"	154		14	8	1	41	73	69	64
	"Spartan"	151	57	11	5	-2	41	72	68	64

Notes: Rate of real growth of per capita GDP: 2% per year.
Enrollment scenarios: The five scenarios for coverage or enrollment are described on pages 16–18.
Resource mobilization scenarios: Scenarios 1–3 assume a budget allocation for education of 20%, 23%, and 26%, respectively; see also pages 43–44.
Shaded cells: Dependency on external financing 35% or less.

CAMEROON

CAMEROON: Enrollments Under Different Policy Scenarios, Base Year and 2020

			Lower secondary			Upper secondary			
		Primary	General	TVET	School-to-work transition program	General	TVET	School-to-work transition program	Tertiary
2003		2,533,204	496,365	n/a	n/a	148,291	35,035	n/a	77,707
2020	ES-1	3,052,188	1,545,955	129,363	0	509,954	87,560	53,436	348,461
	ES-2	3,052,188	1,168,055	155,236	43,785	385,299	66,156	40,374	263,282
	ES-3	3,052,188	1,168,055	155,236	43,785	246,871	80,066	121,814	130,674
	ES-4	3,052,188	893,218	168,172	76,624	204,656	35,140	48,386	95,584
	ES-5	4,179,120				274,242	35,502	139,946	95,584

Note: Rate of real growth of per capita GDP: 2% per year.

CAMEROON: GER and Other Parameters Under Different Policy Scenarios, Base Year and 2020

			Lower secondary GER (%)			Upper secondary GER (%)			Higher education GER (%) and other indicators		
		Primary GER (%)	General	TVET	School-to-work transition program	General	TVET	School-to-work transition program	GER (%)	Students/ 100,000	Unemployment (simulated) (%)
2003		99.6	31.8	n/a	n/a	13.8	3.3	n/a	6.0	485	n/a
2020	ES-1	108.3	85.5	9.5	0.0	38.8	6.7	12.0	20.8	1,711	38
	ES-2	108.3	64.6	11.4	9.5	29.3	5.0	9.0	15.7	1,293	35
	ES-3	108.3	64.6	11.4	9.5	18.8	6.1	27.3	7.8	642	25
	ES-4	108.3	49.4	12.4	16.6	15.6	2.7	10.8	5.7	469	20
	ES-5	100.0				15.6	2.7	31.1	5.7	469	20

Note: Rate of real growth of per capita GDP: 2% per year.

CAMEROON: Teacher Salaries and Per-Student Spending by Level of Education, Base Year and 2020

		Lower secondary			Upper secondary			Higher education			
	Primary	General	TVET	School-to-work transition program	General	TVET	School-to-work transition program	Humanities & social sciences	Sciences	Professional	All
Teacher salaries in multiples of per capita GDP[a]											
2003	3.9	6.5			6.8						
2020 "Generous"	3.0/3.2[b]	4.6			5.9						
"Spartan"		4.2			5.1						
Level of per-student spending in % of per capita GDP[a]											
2003	9	32	55	110	37	62	33	60	120	131	87
2020 "Generous"	13/14[b]	36	90	50	55	140	100	151	242	291	200
"Spartan"		18	90	50	29	140	100	151	242	291	200

Note: Rate of real growth of per capita GDP: 2% per year.

a. After adjustment for wealth, geographic dimension, and/or stimulation of demand.

b. The first number pertains to the 6-year primary cycle (or whatever the duration of the primary cycle) and the second number to the 9-year primary cycle in ES-5.

CAMEROON: Estimated Annual Public Spending on Education and Financing Gap in 2020
2005 US$ million unless otherwise indicated

Policy scenario		Aggregate annual public education spending (recurrent and capital)	Annual recurrent financing gap in **primary or basic education**	Annual recurrent financing gap in **post-primary education** under 3 scenarios for domestic resource mobilization			Annual capital financing gap	Total financing gap as share of total public education spending (%)		
Coverage	Per-student spending at post-primary levels			Scenario 1	Scenario 2	Scenario 3		Scenario 1	Scenario 2	Scenario 3
ES-1	"Generous"	2,263		1,354	1,224	1,093	54	63	55	52
	"Spartan"	1,818		916	785	655	47	54	47	40
ES-2	"Generous"	1,918		1,019	888	757	45	57	50	43
	"Spartan"	1,582		688	557	426	39	48	39	31
ES-3	"Generous"	1,771		874	743	612	43	53	46	39
	"Spartan"	1,464		572	441	310	37	43	35	26
ES-4	"Generous"	1,465		574	443	312	36	43	35	26
	"Spartan"	1,226	27	339	209	78	32	32	22	11
ES-5	"Generous"	1,224		279	149	18	50	32	22	11
	"Spartan"	1,166	67	222	91	–39	49	29	18	7

Notes: Rate of real growth of per capita GDP: 2% per year.
Enrollment scenarios: The five scenarios for coverage or enrollment are described on pages 16–18.
Resource mobilization scenarios: Scenarios 1–3 assume a budget allocation for education of 20%, 23%, and 26%, respectively; see also pages 43–44.
Shaded cells: Dependency on external financing 35% or less.

CENTRAL AFRICAN REPUBLIC

CAMEROON: Enrollments Under Different Policy Scenarios, Base Year and 2020

		Primary	Lower secondary			Upper secondary			Tertiary
			General	TVET	School-to-work transition program	General	TVET	School-to-work transition program	
2004		486,317	60,149	n/a	n/a	18,581	n/a	n/a	9,144
2020	ES-1	821,393	400,576	33,583	0	130,690	22,440	13,766	69,783
	ES-2	821,393	302,657	40,299	11,517	98,743	16,954	10,401	52,725
	ES-3	821,393	302,657	40,299	11,517	25,423	8,245	48,163	13,527
	ES-4	821,393	231,444	43,657	20,155	24,695	4,240	17,895	11,594
	ES-5	1,111,710				33,136	4,294	41,674	11,594

Note: Rate of real growth of per capita GDP: 2% per year.

CENTRAL AFRICAN REPUBLIC: GER and Other Parameters Under Different Policy Scenarios, Base Year and 2020

		Primary GER (%)	Lower secondary GER (%)			Upper secondary GER (%)			Higher education GER (%) and other indicators		
			General	TVET	School-to-work transition program	General	TVET	School-to-work transition program	GER (%)	Students/ 100,000	Unemployment (simulated) (%)
2004		74.8	15.5	n/a	n/a	7.0	n/a	n/a	2.9	229	n/a
2020	ES-1	108.3	85.5	9.5	0.0	38.8	6.7	12.0	16.3	1,407	52
	ES-2	108.3	64.6	11.4	9.5	29.3	5.0	9.0	12.3	1,063	49
	ES-3	108.3	64.6	11.4	9.5	7.6	2.5	41.9	3.2	273	25
	ES-4	108.3	49.4	12.4	16.6	7.3	1.3	15.6	2.7	234	20
	ES-5	100.0				7.3	1.3	35.8	2.7	234	20

Note: Rate of real growth of per capita GDP: 2% per year.

CENTRAL AFRICAN REPUBLIC: Teacher Salaries and Per-Student Spending by Level of Education, Base Year and 2020

		Lower secondary			Upper secondary			Higher education			
	Primary	General	TVET	School-to-work transition program	General	TVET	School-to-work transition program	Humanities & social sciences	Sciences	Professional	All
Teacher salaries in multiples of per capita GDP[a]											
2004	7.0	4.8			5.1						
2020 "Generous"	3.3/3.4[b]	5.0			6.4						
"Spartan"		4.6			5.5						
Level of per-student spending in % of per capita GDP[a]											
2004	12	15	59	110	25	59	33	134	200	238	170
2020 "Generous"	14/16[b]	41	90	50	62	140	100	160	255	308	211
"Spartan"	20	20	90	50	32	140	100	160	255	308	211

Note: Rate of real growth of per capita GDP: 2% per year.

a. After adjustment for wealth, geographic dimension, and/or stimulation of demand.

b. The first number pertains to the 6-year primary cycle (or whatever the duration of the primary cycle) and the second number to the 9-year primary cycle in ES-5.

CENTRAL AFRICAN REPUBLIC: Estimated Annual Public Spending on Education and Financing Gap in 2020
2005 US$ million unless otherwise indicated

Policy scenario		Aggregate annual public education spending (recurrent and capital)	Annual recurrent financing gap in **primary or basic education**	Annual recurrent financing gap in **post-primary education** under 3 scenarios for domestic resource mobilization			Annual capital financing gap	Total financing gap as share of total public education spending (%)		
Coverage	Per-student spending at post-primary levels			Scenario 1	Scenario 2	Scenario 3		Scenario 1	Scenario 2	Scenario 3
ES-1	"Generous"	229		131	122	112	21	73	69	65
	"Spartan"	183		87	77	68	19	67	62	56
ES-2	"Generous"	196		100	91	81	18	69	64	59
	"Spartan"	161		67	57	48	17	62	56	50
ES-3	"Generous"	165		71	61	51	17	63	57	52
	"Spartan"	136		43	34	24	16	55	48	41
ES-4	"Generous"	143		50	40	30	15	57	51	44
	"Spartan"	120	17	28	19	9	14	49	41	33
ES-5	"Generous"	118		14	4	-5	17	48	40	32
	"Spartan"	115	26	11	2	-8	17	47	39	30

Notes: Rate of real growth of per capita GDP: 2% per year.
Enrollment scenarios: The five scenarios for coverage or enrollment are described on pages 16–18.
Resource mobilization scenarios: Scenarios 1–3 assume a budget allocation for education of 20%, 23%, and 26%, respectively; see also pages 43–44.
Shaded cells: Dependency on external financing 35% or less.

CHAD

CHAD: Enrollments Under Different Policy Scenarios, Base Year and 2020

		Primary	Lower secondary			Upper secondary			Tertiary
			General	TVET	School-to-work transition program	General	TVET	School-to-work transition program	
2004		1,212,855	164,752	n/a	n/a	54,212	n/a	n/a	10,636
2020	ES-1	2,791,004	1,217,564	103,366	0	363,327	62,384	40,217	80,549
	ES-2	2,791,004	919,937	124,039	37,128	274,513	47,134	30,387	60,859
	ES-3	2,791,004	919,937	124,039	37,128	82,904	26,888	135,007	46,356
	ES-4	2,791,004	703,481	134,376	64,974	77,976	13,388	50,361	38,471
	ES-5	3,664,376				105,983	13,900	122,945	38,471

Note: Rate of real growth of per capita GDP: 2% per year.

CHAD: GER and Other Parameters Under Different Policy Scenarios, Base Year and 2020

		Primary GER (%)	Lower secondary GER (%)			Upper secondary GER (%)			Higher education GER (%) and other indicators		
			General	TVET	School-to-work transition program	General	TVET	School-to-work transition program	GER (%)	Students/ 100,000	Unemployment (simulated) (%)
2004		76.9	18.7	n/a	n/a	9.4	n/a	n/a	1.6	113	n/a
2020	ES-1	108.3	85.5	9.5	0.0	38.8	6.7	12.0	7.3	541	36
	ES-2	108.3	64.6	11.4	9.5	29.3	5.0	9.0	5.5	409	31
	ES-3	108.3	64.6	11.4	9.5	8.9	2.9	40.2	4.2	312	25
	ES-4	108.3	49.4	12.4	16.6	8.3	1.4	15.0	3.5	259	20
	ES-5	100.0				8.3	1.4	35.2	3.5	259	20

Note: Rate of real growth of per capita GDP: 2% per year.

CHAD: Teacher Salaries and Per-Student Spending by Level of Education, Base Year and 2020

	Primary	Lower secondary			Upper secondary			Higher education			
		General	TVET	School-to-work transition program	General	TVET	School-to-work transition program	Humanities & social sciences	Sciences	Professional	All
Teacher salaries in multiples of per capita GDP[a]											
2004	5.4	4.4			6.8						
2020 "Generous"	3.0/3.2[b]	4.6			5.9						
"Spartan"		4.2			5.1						
Level of per-student spending in % of per capita GDP[a]											
2004	12	19	82	110	25	82	33	80	180	430	182
2020 "Generous"	14/16[b]	41	90	50	62	140	100	202	323	390	267
"Spartan"	20	20	90	50	32	140	100	202	323	390	267

Note: Rate of real growth of per capita GDP: 2% per year.
a. After adjustment for wealth, geographic dimension, and/or stimulation of demand.
b. The first number pertains to the 6-year primary cycle (or whatever the duration of the primary cycle) and the second number to the 9-year primary cycle in ES-5.

CHAD: Estimated Annual Public Spending on Education and Financing Gap in 2020

2005 US$ million unless otherwise indicated

Policy scenario		Aggregate annual public education spending (recurrent and capital)	Annual recurrent financing gap in **primary or basic** education	Annual recurrent financing gap in **post-primary education** under 3 scenarios for domestic resource mobilization			Annual capital financing gap	Total financing gap as share of total public education spending (%)		
Coverage	Per-student spending at post-primary levels			Scenario 1	Scenario 2	Scenario 3		Scenario 1	Scenario 2	Scenario 3
ES-1	"Generous"	877		460	420	380	67	71	66	62
	"Spartan"	684		273	233	193	61	63	57	51
ES-2	"Generous"	763		354	314	274	59	67	61	56
	"Spartan"	617		213	173	132	54	59	52	46
ES-3	"Generous"	724		318	278	238	56	65	59	54
	"Spartan"	600		198	158	118	52	58	51	44
ES-4	"Generous"	628		227	187	147	51	60	53	47
	"Spartan"	532	96	134	94	54	48	52	45	37
ES-5	"Generous"	525		71	31	–9	55	52	44	36
	"Spartan"	512	144	59	19	–21	55	50	43	35

Notes: Rate of real growth of per capita GDP: 2% per year.

Enrollment scenarios: The five scenarios for coverage or enrollment are described on pages 16–18.

Resource mobilization scenarios: Scenarios 1–3 assume a budget allocation for education of 20%, 23%, and 26%, respectively; see also pages 43–44.

Shaded cells: Dependency on external financing 35% or less.

CONGO, DEMOCRATIC REPUBLIC

CONGO, DEM. REP.: Enrollments Under Different Policy Scenarios, Base Year and 2020

			Lower secondary			Upper secondary			
		Primary	General	TVET	School-to-work transition program	General	TVET	School-to-work transition program	Tertiary
2005		8,664,132	510,218	n/a	n/a	530,964	n/a	n/a	127,925
2020	ES-1	16,978,338	3,882,624	830,664	0	3,140,330	661,042	266,697	854,956
	ES-2	16,978,338	2,933,538	996,797	227,635	2,372,694	499,454	201,504	645,967
	ES-3	16,978,338	2,933,538	996,797	227,635	483,232	192,139	978,698	207,306
	ES-4	16,978,338	2,243,294	1,079,864	398,361	491,453	103,451	362,749	186,029
	ES-5	22,356,044				361,213	99,401	782,519	186,029

Note: Rate of real growth of per capita GDP: 2% per year.

CONGO, DEM. REP.: GER and Other Parameters Under Different Policy Scenarios, Base Year and 2020

			Lower secondary GER (%)			Upper secondary GER (%)			Higher education GER (%) and other indicators		
		Primary GER (%)	General	TVET	School-to-work transition program	General	TVET	School-to-work transition program	GER (%)	Students/ 100,000	Unemployment (simulated) (%)
2005		92.6	18.7	n/a	n/a	10.7	n/a	n/a	3.1	229	n/a
2020	ES-1	108.3	85.5	9.5	0.0	38.8	6.7	12.0	12.9	950	53
	ES-2	108.3	64.6	11.4	9.5	29.3	5.0	9.0	9.8	718	49
	ES-3	108.3	64.6	11.4	9.5	6.0	1.9	43.9	3.1	230	25
	ES-4	108.3	49.4	12.4	16.6	6.1	1.0	16.3	2.8	207	20
	ES-5	100.0				6.1	1.0	36.5	2.8	207	20

Note: Rate of real growth of per capita GDP: 2% per year.

CONGO, DEM. REP.: Teacher Salaries and Per-Student Spending by Level of Education, Base Year and 2020

		Lower secondary			Upper secondary			Higher education			
	Primary	General	TVET	School-to-work transition program	General	TVET	School-to-work transition program	Humanities & social sciences	Sciences	Professional	All
Teacher salaries in multiples of per capita GDP[a]											
2005	2.2	2.4			2.4						
2020 "Generous"	3.9/4.1[b]	6.0			7.7						
"Spartan"	5.5	5.5			6.6						
Level of per-student spending in % of per capita GDP[a]											
2005	8	19	140	110	19	160	33	164	187	248	188
2020 "Generous"	22/26[b]	69	90	50	111	140	100	353	565	681	467
"Spartan"	33	33	90	50	55	140	100	353	565	681	467

Note: Rate of real growth of per capita GDP: 2% per year.
a. After adjustment for wealth, geographic dimension, and/or stimulation of demand.
b. The first number pertains to the 6-year primary cycle (or whatever the duration of the primary cycle) and the second number to the 9-year primary cycle in ES-5.

CONGO, DEM. REP.: Estimated Annual Public Spending on Education and Financing Gap in 2020
2005 US$ million unless otherwise indicated

Policy scenario		Aggregate annual public education spending (recurrent and capital)	Annual recurrent financing gap in **primary or basic education**	Annual recurrent financing gap in **post-primary education** under 3 scenarios for domestic resource mobilization			Annual capital financing gap	Total financing gap as share of total public education spending (%)		
Coverage	Per-student spending at post-primary levels			Scenario 1	Scenario 2	Scenario 3		Scenario 1	Scenario 2	Scenario 3
ES-1	"Generous"	2,256		1,237	1,174	1,112	262	82	80	77
	"Spartan"	1,847		853	790	727	238	78	75	72
ES-2	"Generous"	1,941		957	895	832	227	80	76	73
	"Spartan"	1,632		667	604	541	209	76	72	68
ES-3	"Generous"	1,520		559	496	433	205	74	70	66
	"Spartan"	1,320		373	311	248	191	70	65	60
ES-4	"Generous"	1,366		422	359	297	188	71	66	62
	"Spartan"	1,207	359	274	211	148	177	67	62	57
ES-5	"Generous"	1,356		144	81	18	271	71	66	61
	"Spartan"	1,336	544	124	61	-2	271	70	66	61

Notes: Rate of real growth of per capita GDP: 2% per year.
Enrollment scenarios: The five scenarios for coverage or enrollment are described on pages 16–18.
Resource mobilization scenarios: Scenarios 1–3 assume a budget allocation for education of 20%, 23%, and 26%, respectively, see also pages 43–44.
Shaded cells: Dependency on external financing 35% or less.

CONGO, REPUBLIC

CONGO, REP.: Enrollments Under Different Policy Scenarios, Base Year and 2020

| | | | Lower secondary | | | Upper secondary | | | |
		Primary	General	TVET	School-to-work transition program	General	TVET	School-to-work transition program	Tertiary
	2005	564,457	170,421	n/a	n/a	37,720	21,411	5,567	12,676
2020	ES-1	1,191,944	530,208	44,924	0	160,100	27,489	17,625	65,154
	ES-2	1,191,944	400,601	53,909	16,017	120,964	20,770	13,316	49,228
	ES-3	1,191,944	400,601	53,909	16,017	190,278	61,712	0	105,811
	ES-4	1,191,944	306,342	58,401	28,031	145,443	24,973	0	71,363
	ES-5	1,573,143				197,396	25,859	30,174	71,363

Note: Rate of real growth of per capita GDP: 2% per year.

CONGO, REP.: GER and Other Parameters Under Different Policy Scenarios, Base Year and 2020

| | | | Lower secondary GER (%) | | | Upper secondary GER (%) | | | Higher education GER (%) and other indicators | | |
		Primary GER (%)	General	TVET	School-to-work transition program	General	TVET	School-to-work transition program	GER (%)	Students/ 100,000	Unemployment (simulated) (%)
	2005	85.7	46.6	n/a	n/a	15.5	8.8	6.4	4.4	327	n/a
2020	ES-1	108.3	85.5	9.5	0.0	38.8	6.7	12.0	13.4	1,024	19
	ES-2	108.3	64.6	11.4	9.5	29.3	5.0	9.0	10.1	774	15
	ES-3	108.3	64.6	11.4	9.5	46.2	15.0	0.0	21.8	1,664	25
	ES-4	108.3	49.4	12.4	16.6	35.3	6.1	0.0	14.7	1,122	20
	ES-5	100.0				35.3	6.1	19.8	14.7	1,122	20

Note: Rate of real growth of per capita GDP: 2% per year.

CONGO, REP.: Teacher Salaries and Per-Student Spending by Level of Education, Base Year and 2020

		Lower secondary			Upper secondary			Higher education			
	Primary	General	TVET	School-to-work transition program	General	TVET	School-to-work transition program	Humanities & social sciences	Sciences	Professional	All
Teacher salaries in multiples of per capita GDP[a]											
2005	1.8	2.3			2.7						
2020 "Generous"	3.0/3.2[b]	4.6			5.9						
"Spartan"		4.2			5.1						
Level of per-student spending in % of per capita GDP[a]											
2005	7	12	24	110	36	26	33	126	241	329	194
2020 "Generous"	12/14[b]	35	90	50	55	140	100	151	242	291	200
"Spartan"	18	18	90	50	29	140	100	151	242	291	200

Note: Rate of real growth of per capita GDP: 2% per year.
a. After adjustment for wealth, geographic dimension, and/or stimulation of demand.
b. The first number pertains to the 6-year primary cycle (or whatever the duration of the primary cycle) and the second number to the 9-year primary cycle in ES-5.

CONGO, REP.: Estimated Annual Public Spending on Education and Financing Gap in 2020

2005 US$ million unless otherwise indicated

Policy scenario		Aggregate annual public education spending (recurrent and capital)	Annual recurrent financing gap in **primary or basic education**	Annual recurrent financing gap in **post-primary education** under 3 scenarios for domestic resource mobilization			Annual capital financing gap	Total financing gap as share of total public education spending (%)		
Coverage	Per-student spending at post-primary levels			Scenario 1	Scenario 2	Scenario 3		Scenario 1	Scenario 2	Scenario 3
ES-1	"Generous"	1,075		569	500	431	31	59	53	46
	"Spartan"	852		349	280	211	28	49	41	32
ES-2	"Generous"	930		428	359	290	27	53	45	38
	"Spartan"	762		262	193	124	25	43	33	24
ES-3	"Generous"	1,198		694	625	556	28	63	58	52
	"Spartan"	1,007		507	437	368	26	57	50	43
ES-4	"Generous"	951		451	382	313	25	54	47	39
	"Spartan"	806	37	307	238	169	23	46	37	28
ES-5	"Generous"	843		321	252	183	28	48	40	32
	"Spartan"	781	57	259	190	121	28	44	35	26

Notes: Rate of real growth of per capita GDP: 2% per year.

Enrollment scenarios: The five scenarios for coverage or enrollment are described on pages 16–18.

Resource mobilization scenarios: Scenarios 1–3 assume a budget allocation for education of 20%, 23%, and 26%, respectively; see also pages 43–44.

Shaded cells: Dependency on external financing 35% or less.

CÔTE D'IVOIRE

CÔTE D'IVOIRE: Enrollments Under Different Policy Scenarios, Base Year and 2020

		Primary	Lower secondary			Upper secondary			Tertiary
			General	TVET	School-to-work transition program	General	TVET	School-to-work transition program	
	2000	1,916,047	393,089	n/a	n/a	126,394	n/a	n/a	110,472
2020	ES-1	3,587,016	1,787,143	149,711	0	586,097	100,633	61,564	731,005
	ES-2	3,587,016	1,350,286	179,653	50,980	442,829	76,034	46,515	552,315
	ES-3	3,587,016	1,350,286	179,653	50,980	254,701	82,606	153,178	135,146
	ES-4	3,587,016	1,032,571	194,625	89,216	214,050	36,753	59,873	100,214
	ES-5	4,886,999				287,007	37,169	165,727	100,214

Note: Rate of real growth of per capita GDP: 2% per year.

CÔTE D'IVOIRE: GER and Other Parameters Under Different Policy Scenarios, Base Year and 2020

		Primary GER (%)	Lower secondary GER (%)			Upper secondary GER (%)			Higher education GER (%) and other indicators		
			General	TVET	School-to-work transition program	General	TVET	School-to-work transition program	GER (%)	Students/ 100,000	Unemployment (simulated) (%)
	2000	66.7	22.0	n/a	n/a	10.2	n/a	n/a	7.5	619	n/a
2020	ES-1	108.3	85.5	9.5	0.0	38.8	6.7	12.0	37.9	3,132	47
	ES-2	108.3	64.6	11.4	9.5	29.3	5.0	9.0	28.7	2,366	44
	ES-3	108.3	64.6	11.4	9.5	16.9	5.5	29.8	7.0	579	25
	ES-4	108.3	49.4	12.4	16.6	14.2	2.4	11.6	5.2	429	20
	ES-5	100.0				14.2	2.4	31.9	5.2	429	20

Note: Rate of real growth of per capita GDP: 2% per year.

CÔTE D'IVOIRE: Teacher Salaries and Per-Student Spending by Level of Education, Base Year and 2020

		Lower secondary			Upper secondary			Higher education			
	Primary	General	TVET	School-to-work transition program	General	TVET	School-to-work transition program	Humanities & social sciences	Sciences	Professional	All
Teacher salaries in multiples of per capita GDP[a]											
2000	4.8	7.7			8.9						
2020 "Generous"	3.0/3.2[b]	4.6			5.9						
"Spartan"		4.2			5.1						
Level of per-student spending in % of per capita GDP[a]											
2000	15	34	110	110	63	110	33	83	94	125	95
2020 "Generous"	13/14[b]	36	90	50	55	140	100	151	242	291	200
"Spartan"	18	18	90	50	29	140	100	151	242	291	200

Note: Rate of real growth of per capita GDP: 2% per year.

a. After adjustment for wealth, geographic dimension, and/or stimulation of demand.

b. The first number pertains to the 6-year primary cycle (or whatever the duration of the primary cycle) and the second number to the 9-year primary cycle in ES-5.

CÔTE D'IVOIRE: Estimated Annual Public Spending on Education and Financing Gap in 2020

2005 US$ million unless otherwise indicated

Policy scenario		Aggregate annual public education spending (recurrent and capital)	Annual recurrent financing gap in **primary or basic education**	Annual recurrent financing gap in **post-primary education** under 3 scenarios for domestic resource mobilization			Annual capital financing gap	Total financing gap as share of total public education spending (%)		
Coverage	Per-student spending at post-primary levels			Scenario 1	Scenario 2	Scenario 3		Scenario 1	Scenario 2	Scenario 3
ES-1	"Generous"	2,985		1,935	1,777	1,619	62	66	61	56
	"Spartan"	2,501		1,459	1,301	1,143	54	60	54	47
ES-2	"Generous"	2,486		1,446	1,288	1,130	52	60	53	47
	"Spartan"	2,121		1,086	928	770	46	53	45	38
ES-3	"Generous"	1,894		857	699	541	50	47	39	30
	"Spartan"	1,566		534	376	218	44	36	26	16
ES-4	"Generous"	1,579		547	389	231	43	37	27	17
	"Spartan"	1,324	−13	296	138	−20	39	24	12	0
ES-5	"Generous"	1,306		249	91	−67	49	23	11	−1
	"Spartan"	1,249	6	193	35	−123	49	20	7	−5

Notes: Rate of real growth of per capita GDP: 2% per year.
Enrollment scenarios: The five scenarios for coverage or enrollment are described on pages 16–18.
Resource mobilization scenarios: Scenarios 1–3 assume a budget allocation for education of 20%, 23%, and 26%, respectively, see also pages 43–44.
Shaded cells: Dependency on external financing 35% or less.

ERITREA

ERITREA: Enrollments Under Different Policy Scenarios, Base Year and 2020

		Primary	Lower secondary			Upper secondary			Tertiary
			General	TVET	School-to-work transition program	General	TVET	School-to-work transition program	
	2005	428,766	142,485	n/a	n/a	92,156	n/a	n/a	5,068
2020	ES-1	941,442	416,018	60,993	0	233,070	30,383	19,025	15,996
	ES-2	941,442	314,324	73,192	15,990	176,097	22,956	14,375	12,086
	ES-3	941,442	314,324	73,192	15,990	39,356	9,691	68,618	16,228
	ES-4	941,442	240,366	79,291	27,982	39,267	5,119	25,454	14,287
	ES-5	1,511,055				29,094	4,996	56,362	14,287

Note: Rate of real growth of per capita GDP: 2% per year.

ERITREA: GER and Other Parameters Under Different Policy Scenarios, Base Year and 2020

		Primary GER (%)	Lower secondary GER (%)			Upper secondary GER (%)			Higher education GER (%) and other indicators		
			General	TVET	School-to-work transition program	General	TVET	School-to-work transition program	GER (%)	Students/ 100,000	Unemployment (simulated) (%)
	2005	73.9	46.1	n/a	n/a	24.7	n/a	n/a	1.5	120	n/a
2020	ES-1	108.3	85.5	9.5	0.0	38.8	6.7	12.0	3.1	243	25
	ES-2	108.3	64.6	11.4	9.5	29.3	5.0	9.0	2.3	184	9
	ES-3	108.3	64.6	11.4	9.5	6.6	2.1	43.2	3.1	246	25
	ES-4	108.3	49.4	12.4	16.6	6.5	1.1	16.0	2.7	217	20
	ES-5	100.0				6.5	1.1	36.3	2.7	217	20

Note: Rate of real growth of per capita GDP: 2% per year.

ERITREA: Teacher Salaries and Per-Student Spending by Level of Education, Base Year and 2020

		Lower secondary			Upper secondary			Higher education			
	Primary	General	TVET	School-to-work transition program	General	TVET	School-to-work transition program	Humanities & social sciences	Sciences	Professional	All
Teacher salaries in multiples of per capita GDP[a]											
2005	3.9	9.9			11.8						
2020 "Generous"	3.6/3.8[b]	5.5			7.1						
"Spartan"		5.1			6.2						
Level of per-student spending in % of per capita GDP[a]											
2005	12	25	140	110	35	160	33	320	365	485	368
2020 "Generous"	18/22[b]	53	90	50	81	140	100	239	382	461	316
"Spartan"		26	90	50	42	140	100	239	382	461	316

Note: Rate of real growth of per capita GDP: 2% per year.
a. After adjustment for wealth, geographic dimension, and/or stimulation of demand.
b. The first number pertains to the 6-year primary cycle (or whatever the duration of the primary cycle) and the second number to the 9-year primary cycle in ES-5.

ERITREA: Estimated Annual Public Spending on Education and Financing Gap in 2020
2005 US$ million unless otherwise indicated

Policy scenario				Annual recurrent financing gap in **post-primary education** under 3 scenarios for domestic resource mobilization			Annual capital financing gap	Total financing gap as share of total public education spending (%)		
Coverage	Per-student spending at post-primary levels	Aggregate annual public education spending (recurrent and capital)	Annual recurrent financing gap in **primary or basic education**	Scenario 1	Scenario 2	Scenario 3		Scenario 1	Scenario 2	Scenario 3
ES-1	"Generous"	200		104	95	87	21	74	70	66
	"Spartan"	151		57	49	41	19	66	60	55
ES-2	"Generous"	173		80	72	64	18	70	65	60
	"Spartan"	136		45	37	29	16	62	56	50
ES-3	"Generous"	157		66	58	50	16	67	62	57
	"Spartan"	130		41	33	24	15	60	54	48
ES-4	"Generous"	137		48	40	32	14	62	56	50
	"Spartan"	116	23	28	20	12	13	55	48	41
ES-5	"Generous"	134		22	13	5	22	61	55	49
	"Spartan"	131	38	20	11	3	22	61	54	48

Notes: Rate of real growth of per capita GDP: 2% per year.

Enrollment scenarios: The five scenarios for coverage or enrollment are described on pages 16–18.

Resource mobilization scenarios: Scenarios 1–3 assume a budget allocation for education of 20%, 23%, and 26%, respectively, see also pages 43–44.

Shaded cells: Dependency on external financing 35% or less.

ETHIOPIA

ETHIOPIA: Enrollments Under Different Policy Scenarios, Base Year and 2020

			Lower secondary			Upper secondary			
		Primary	General	TVET	School-to-work transition program	General	TVET	School-to-work transition program	Tertiary
2002		5,954,992	2,396,728	n/a	n/a	684,349	n/a	n/a	101,829
2020	ES-1	12,200,467	8,899,888	988,876	0	3,728,775	165,024	302,207	567,591
	ES-2	12,200,467	6,724,360	1,186,652	259,755	2,817,297	124,685	228,334	428,847
	ES-3	12,200,467	6,724,360	1,186,652	259,755	603,370	50,440	1,098,916	247,023
	ES-4	12,200,467	5,142,158	1,285,539	454,571	614,314	27,188	406,418	221,915
	ES-5	24,145,693				455,971	26,640	899,173	221,915

Note: Rate of real growth of per capita GDP: 2% per year.

ETHIOPIA: GER and Other Parameters Under Different Policy Scenarios, Base Year and 2020

			Lower secondary GER (%)			Upper secondary GER (%)			Higher education GER (%) and other indicators		
		Primary GER (%)	General	TVET	School-to-work transition program	General	TVET	School-to-work transition program	GER (%)	Students/ 100,000	Unemployment (simulated) (%)
2002		69.1	31.0	n/a	n/a	10.1	n/a	n/a	1.8	135	n/a
2020	ES-1	108.3	85.5	9.5	0.0	38.8	6.7	12.0	6.6	527	44
	ES-2	108.3	64.6	11.4	9.5	29.3	5.0	9.0	5.0	398	39
	ES-3	108.3	64.6	11.4	9.5	6.3	2.0	43.5	2.9	229	25
	ES-4	108.3	49.4	12.4	16.6	6.4	1.1	16.1	2.6	206	20
	ES-5	100.0				6.4	1.1	36.3	2.6	206	20

Note: Rate of real growth of per capita GDP: 2% per year.

ETHIOPIA: Teacher Salaries and Per-Student Spending by Level of Education, Base Year and 2020

		Lower secondary			Upper secondary			Higher education			
	Primary	General	TVET	School-to-work transition program	General	TVET	School-to-work transition program	Humanities & social sciences	Sciences	Professional	All
Teacher salaries in multiples of per capita GDP[a]											
2002	6.8	8.1			11.9						
2020 "Generous"	3.9/4.2[b]	6.0			7.7						
"Spartan"		5.5			6.7						
Level of per-student spending in % of per capita GDP[a]											
2002	11	21	284	110	40	284	33	973	1,371	1,371	1,132
2020 "Generous"	22/27[b]	64	90	50	101	140	100	305	487	588	403
"Spartan"	31	31	90	50	51	140	100	305	487	588	403

Note: Rate of real growth of per capita GDP: 2% per year.
a. After adjustment for wealth, geographic dimension, and/or stimulation of demand.
b. The first number pertains to the 6-year primary cycle (or whatever the duration of the primary cycle) and the second number to the 9-year primary cycle in ES-5.

ETHIOPIA: Estimated Annual Public Spending on Education and Financing Gap in 2020
2005 US$ million unless otherwise indicated

Coverage	Policy scenario — Per-student spending at post-primary levels	Aggregate annual public education spending (recurrent and capital)	Annual recurrent financing gap in **primary or basic education**	Annual recurrent financing gap in **post-primary education** under 3 scenarios for domestic resource mobilization			Annual capital financing gap	Total financing gap as share of total public education spending (%)		
				Scenario 1	Scenario 2	Scenario 3		Scenario 1	Scenario 2	Scenario 3
ES-1	"Generous"	2,280		1,276	1,205	1,133	337	80	77	74
	"Spartan"	1,641		678	607	536	296	72	68	64
ES-2	"Generous"	1,917		969	898	826	281	76	73	69
	"Spartan"	1,434		518	446	375	250	68	63	58
ES-3	"Generous"	1,679		761	689	618	252	73	69	65
	"Spartan"	1,305		414	343	271	224	65	60	54
ES-4	"Generous"	1,451		565	493	422	220	69	64	59
	"Spartan"	1,158	214	293	221	150	199	61	55	49
ES-5	"Generous"	1,488		303	231	160	346	70	65	60
	"Spartan"	1,465	386	281	210	138	346	69	64	59

Notes: Rate of real growth of per capita GDP: 2% per year.
Enrollment scenarios: The five scenarios for coverage or enrollment are described on pages 16–18.
Resource mobilization scenarios: Scenarios 1–3 assume a budget allocation for education of 20%, 23%, and 26%, respectively; see also pages 43–44.
Shaded cells: Dependency on external financing 35% or less.

THE GAMBIA

THE GAMBIA: Enrollments Under Different Policy Scenarios, Base Year and 2020

| | | | Lower secondary | | | Upper secondary | | | |
		Primary	General	TVET	School-to-work transition program	General	TVET	School-to-work transition program	Tertiary
	2001	223,219	53,193	n/a	n/a	26,842	n/a	n/a	2,000
2020	ES-1	303,882	116,115	12,902	0	50,863	8,733	5,363	6,708
	ES-2	303,882	87,732	15,482	4,374	38,430	6,598	4,052	5,068
	ES-3	303,882	87,732	15,482	4,374	11,967	3,881	17,844	6,374
	ES-4	303,882	67,089	16,772	7,654	11,287	1,938	6,643	5,305
	ES-5	416,314				11,287	1,938	15,712	5,305

Note: Rate of real growth of per capita GDP: 2% per year.

THE GAMBIA: GER and Other Parameters Under Different Policy Scenarios, Base Year and 2020

| | | Primary GER (%) | Lower secondary GER (%) | | | Upper secondary GER (%) | | | Higher education GER (%) and other indicators | | |
			General	TVET	School-to-work transition program	General	TVET	School-to-work transition program	GER (%)	Students/ 100,000	Unemployment (simulated) (%)
	2001		101.0	54.7	n/a	n/a	30.1	n/a	n/a	1.9	136
2020	ES-1	108.3	85.5	9.5	0.0	38.8	6.7	12.0	4.2	324	26
	ES-2	108.3	64.6	11.4	9.5	29.3	5.0	9.0	3.2	245	19
	ES-3	108.3	64.6	11.4	9.5	9.1	3.0	39.8	4.0	308	25
	ES-4	108.3	49.4	12.4	16.6	8.6	1.5	14.8	3.3	256	20
	ES-5	100.0				8.6	1.5	35.1	3.3	256	20

Note: Rate of real growth of per capita GDP: 2% per year.

THE GAMBIA: Teacher Salaries and Per-Student Spending by Level of Education, Base Year and 2020

		Lower secondary			Upper secondary			Higher education			
	Primary	General	TVET	School-to-work transition program	General	TVET	School-to-work transition program	Humanities & social sciences	Sciences	Professional	All
Teacher salaries in multiples of per capita GDP[a]											
2001	4.5	6.5			6.5						
2020 "Generous"	3.0/3.2[b]	4.6			5.9						
"Spartan"		4.2			5.1						
Level of per-student spending in % of per capita GDP[a]											
2001	16	26	140	110	47	160	33	284	324	431	327
2020 "Generous"	13/14[b]	36	90	50	55	140	100	151	242	291	200
"Spartan"	18	18	90	50	29	140	100	151	242	291	200

Note: Rate of real growth of per capita GDP: 2% per year.
a. After adjustment for wealth, geographic dimension, and/or stimulation of demand.
b. The first number pertains to the 6-year primary cycle (or whatever the duration of the primary cycle) and the second number to the 9-year primary cycle in ES-5.

THE GAMBIA: Estimated Annual Public Spending on Education and Financing Gap in 2020
2005 US$ million unless otherwise indicated

Policy scenario		Aggregate annual public education spending (recurrent and capital)	Annual recurrent financing gap in **primary or basic education**	Annual recurrent financing gap in **post-primary education** under 3 scenarios for domestic resource mobilization			Annual capital financing gap	Total financing gap as share of total public education spending (%)		
Coverage	Per-student spending at post-primary levels			Scenario 1	Scenario 2	Scenario 3		Scenario 1	Scenario 2	Scenario 3
ES-1	"Generous"	81		36	30	24	4	51	44	36
	"Spartan"	64		20	14	7	4	38	28	19
ES-2	"Generous"	71		27	21	15	3	44	36	27
	"Spartan"	58		15	8	2	3	32	21	11
ES-3	"Generous"	69		26	19	13	3	43	34	25
	"Spartan"	59		16	9	3	3	33	22	12
ES-4	"Generous"	59		16	10	4	3	34	23	13
	"Spartan"	51	1	8	2	-4	2	23	11	-1
ES-5	"Generous"	51		6	-1	-7	4	23	11	-1
	"Spartan"	50	3	5	-2	-8	4	22	9	-3

Notes: Rate of real growth of per capita GDP: 2% per year.
Enrollment scenarios: The five scenarios for coverage or enrollment are described on pages 16–18.
Resource mobilization scenarios: Scenarios 1–3 assume a budget allocation for education of 20%, 23%, and 26%, respectively, see also pages 43–44.
Shaded cells: Dependency on external financing 35% or less.

GHANA

GHANA: Enrollments Under Different Policy Scenarios, Base Year and 2020

			Lower secondary			Upper secondary			
		Primary	General	TVET	School-to-work transition program	General	TVET	School-to-work transition program	Tertiary
	2001	3,059,751	847,986	n/a	n/a	219,450	10,525	n/a	75,000
2020	ES-1	4,090,999	1,552,114	172,457	0	683,918	117,429	71,756	244,256
	ES-2	4,090,999	1,172,709	206,949	58,549	516,738	88,724	54,216	184,549
	ES-3	4,090,999	1,172,709	206,949	58,549	155,473	50,424	241,139	82,400
	ES-4	4,090,999	896,777	224,194	102,461	149,206	25,619	89,382	69,775
	ES-5	5,591,645				149,206	25,619	210,715	69,775

Note: Rate of real growth of per capita GDP: 2% per year.

GHANA: GER and Other Parameters Under Different Policy Scenarios, Base Year and 2020

			Lower secondary GER (%)			Upper secondary GER (%)			Higher education GER (%) and other indicators		
		Primary GER (%)	General	TVET	School-to-work transition program	General	TVET	School-to-work transition program	GER (%)	Students/ 100,000	Unemployment (simulated) (%)
	2001	93.0	54.4	n/a	n/a	14.9	0.7	n/a	4.3	346	n/a
2020	ES-1	108.3	85.5	9.5	0.0	38.8	6.7	12.0	11.0	848	44
	ES-2	108.3	64.6	11.4	9.5	29.3	5.0	9.0	8.3	641	40
	ES-3	108.3	64.6	11.4	9.5	8.8	3.1	40.2	3.7	286	25
	ES-4	108.3	49.4	12.4	16.6	8.5	1.5	14.9	3.2	242	20
	ES-5	100.0				8.5	1.5	35.2	3.2	242	20

Note: Rate of real growth of per capita GDP: 2% per year.

GHANA: Teacher Salaries and Per-Student Spending by Level of Education, Base Year and 2020

	Primary	Lower secondary			Upper secondary			Higher education			
		General	TVET	School-to-work transition program	General	TVET	School-to-work transition program	Humanities & social sciences	Sciences	Professional	All
Teacher salaries in multiples of per capita GDP[a]											
2001	3.9	3.9			5.9						
2020 "Generous"	3.1/3.3[b]	4.8			6.1						
"Spartan"		4.3			5.3						
Level of per-student spending in % of per capita GDP[a]											
2001	16	30	140	110	83	160	33	277	316	419	318
2020 "Generous"	14/16[b]	40	90	50	63	140	100	191	305	368	252
"Spartan"	20	20	90	50	33	140	100	191	305	368	252

Note: Rate of real growth of per capita GDP: 2% per year.
a. After adjustment for wealth, geographic dimension, and/or stimulation of demand.
b. The first number pertains to the 6-year primary cycle (or whatever the duration of the primary cycle) and the second number to the 9-year primary cycle in ES-5.

GHANA: Estimated Annual Public Spending on Education and Financing Gap in 2020
2005 US$ million unless otherwise indicated

Policy scenario		Aggregate annual public education spending (recurrent and capital)	Annual recurrent financing gap in **primary or basic education**	Annual recurrent financing gap in **post-primary education** under 3 scenarios for domestic resource mobilization			Annual capital financing gap	Total financing gap as share of total public education spending (%)		
Coverage	Per-student spending at post-primary levels			Scenario 1	Scenario 2	Scenario 3		Scenario 1	Scenario 2	Scenario 3
ES-1	"Generous"	1,109		616	552	488	27	63	58	52
	"Spartan"	892		400	336	272	26	54	47	40
ES-2	"Generous"	958		467	403	339	25	58	51	44
	"Spartan"	794		304	240	176	24	49	41	33
ES-3	"Generous"	836		349	285	220	22	51	44	36
	"Spartan"	708		220	156	92	22	43	34	24
ES-4	"Generous"	724		237	172	108	22	44	35	26
	"Spartan"	623	60	135	71	7	22	35	25	14
ES-5	"Generous"	642		86	22	-42	46	37	27	17
	"Spartan"	628	103	72	8	-56	46	35	25	15

Notes: Rate of real growth of per capita GDP: 2% per year.
Enrollment scenarios: The five scenarios for coverage or enrollment are described on pages 16–18.
Resource mobilization scenarios: Scenarios 1–3 assume a budget allocation for education of 20%, 23%, and 26%, respectively, see also pages 43–44.
Shaded cells: Dependency on external financing 35% or less.

GUINEA

GUINEA: Enrollments Under Different Policy Scenarios, Base Year and 2020

| | | | Lower secondary | | | Upper secondary | | | |
		Primary	General	TVET	School-to-work transition program	General	TVET	School-to-work transition program	Tertiary
2005		1,474,640	306,211	n/a	n/a	119,229	n/a	n/a	23,107
2020	ES-1	2,246,231	1,058,597	89,194	0	332,355	57,066	35,819	73,429
	ES-2	2,246,231	799,829	107,033	31,079	251,113	43,116	27,063	55,480
	ES-3	2,246,231	799,829	107,033	31,079	67,703	21,958	123,932	36,858
	ES-4	2,246,231	611,634	115,952	54,389	65,586	11,261	46,003	31,505
	ES-5	3,012,329				88,522	11,539	109,020	31,505

Note: Rate of real growth of per capita GDP: 2% per year.

GUINEA: GER and Other Parameters Under Different Policy Scenarios, Base Year and 2020

| | | Primary GER (%) | Lower secondary GER (%) | | | Upper secondary GER (%) | | | Higher education GER (%) and other indicators | | |
			General	TVET	School-to-work transition program	General	TVET	School-to-work transition program	GER (%)	Students/ 100,000	Unemployment (simulated) (%)
2005		99.1	36.1	n/a	n/a	21.5	n/a	n/a	3.5	251	n/a
2020	ES-1	108.3	85.5	9.5	0.0	38.8	6.7	12.0	7.1	549	39
	ES-2	108.3	64.6	11.4	9.5	29.3	5.0	9.0	5.3	415	34
	ES-3	108.3	64.6	11.4	9.5	7.9	2.6	41.4	3.5	276	25
	ES-4	108.3	49.4	12.4	16.6	7.7	1.3	15.4	3.0	236	20
	ES-5	100.0				7.7	1.3	35.6	3.0	236	20

Note: Rate of real growth of per capita GDP: 2% per year.

GUINEA: Teacher Salaries and Per-Student Spending by Level of Education, Base Year and 2020

	Primary	Lower secondary			Upper secondary			Higher education			
		General	TVET	School-to-work transition program	General	TVET	School-to-work transition program	Humanities & social sciences	Sciences	Professional	All
Teacher salaries in multiples of per capita GDP[a]											
2005	1.7	2.9			2.9						
2020 "Generous"	3.2/3.4[b]	4.9			6.3						
"Spartan"		4.5			5.5						
Level of per-student spending in % of per capita GDP[a]											
2005	6	11	66	110	9	66	33	114	130	172	131
2020 "Generous"	14/16[b]	40	90	50	59	140	100	151	242	291	200
"Spartan"	20	20	90	50	31	140	100	151	242	291	200

Note: Rate of real growth of per capita GDP: 2% per year.
a. After adjustment for wealth, geographic dimension, and/or stimulation of demand.
b. The first number pertains to the 6-year primary cycle (or whatever the duration of the primary cycle) and the second number to the 9-year primary cycle in ES-5.

GUINEA: Estimated Annual Public Spending on Education and Financing Gap in 2020

2005 US$ million unless otherwise indicated

Policy scenario		Aggregate annual public education spending (recurrent and capital)	Annual recurrent financing gap in **primary or basic education**	Annual recurrent financing gap in **post-primary education** under 3 scenarios for domestic resource mobilization			Annual capital financing gap	Total financing gap as share of total public education spending (%)		
Coverage	Per-student spending at post-primary levels			Scenario 1	Scenario 2	Scenario 3		Scenario 1	Scenario 2	Scenario 3
ES-1	"Generous"	554		272	241	211	54	65	60	54
	"Spartan"	433		156	125	95	49	55	48	41
ES-2	"Generous"	481		206	175	144	47	60	53	47
	"Spartan"	389		118	88	57	43	50	42	34
ES-3	"Generous"	447		175	145	114	44	57	50	43
	"Spartan"	370		102	72	41	40	48	39	31
ES-4	"Generous"	387		119	89	58	39	50	42	34
	"Spartan"	327	34	63	32	1	36	41	31	22
ES-5	"Generous"	322		31	1	−30	44	40	30	21
	"Spartan"	315	53	24	−7	−37	44	38	29	19

Notes: Rate of real growth of per capita GDP: 2% per year.
Enrollment scenarios: The five scenarios for coverage or enrollment are described on pages 16–18.
Resource mobilization scenarios: Scenarios 1–3 assume a budget allocation for education of 20%, 23%, and 26%, respectively, see also pages 43–44.
Shaded cells: Dependency on external financing 35% or less.

GUINEA-BISSAU

GUINEA-BISSAU: Enrollments Under Different Policy Scenarios, Base Year and 2020

		Primary	Lower secondary			Upper secondary			Tertiary
			General	TVET	School-to-work transition program	General	TVET	School-to-work transition program	
2002		206,875	29,023	n/a	n/a	9,850	n/a	n/a	1,384
2020	ES-1	465,147	156,913	11,844	0	43,143	10,901	7,044	5,820
	ES-2	465,147	118,556	14,213	6,241	32,597	8,236	5,322	4,398
	ES-3	465,147	118,556	14,213	6,241	7,272	3,471	25,415	5,998
	ES-4	465,147	90,661	15,397	10,922	7,293	1,843	9,417	5,307
	ES-5	612,890				7,293	1,843	21,328	5,307

Note: Rate of real growth of per capita GDP: 2% per year.

GUINEA-BISSAU: GER and Other Parameters Under Different Policy Scenarios, Base Year and 2020

		Primary GER (%)	Lower secondary GER (%)			Upper secondary GER (%)			Higher education GER (%) and other indicators		
			General	TVET	School-to-work transition program	General	TVET	School-to-work transition program	GER (%)	Students/ 100,000	Unemployment (simulated) (%)
2002		80.4	27.0	n/a	n/a	15.2	n/a	n/a	1.3	90	n/a
2020	ES-1	108.3	85.5	9.5	0.0	38.8	6.7	12.0	3.2	235	24
	ES-2	108.3	64.6	11.4	9.5	29.3	5.0	9.0	2.4	177	5
	ES-3	108.3	64.6	11.4	9.5	6.5	2.1	43.2	3.3	242	25
	ES-4	108.3	49.4	12.4	16.6	6.6	1.1	16.0	2.9	214	20
	ES-5	100.0				6.6	1.1	36.2	2.9	214	20

Note: Rate of real growth of per capita GDP: 2% per year.

GUINEA-BISSAU: Teacher Salaries and Per-Student Spending by Level of Education, Base Year and 2020

		Lower secondary			Upper secondary			Higher education			
	Primary	General	TVET	School-to-work transition program	General	TVET	School-to-work transition program	Humanities & social sciences	Sciences	Professional	All
Teacher salaries in multiples of per capita GDP[a]											
2002	1.9	2.2			2.2						
2020 "Generous"	3.7/3.9[b]	5.7			7.3						
"Spartan"	5.2	5.2			6.3						
Level of per-student spending in % of per capita GDP[a]											
2002	7	14	344	110	14	344	33	92	105	140	106
2020 "Generous"	17/20[b]	50	90	50	77	140	100	205	328	396	271
"Spartan"	25	25	90	50	40	140	100	205	328	396	271

Note: Rate of real growth of per capita GDP: 2% per year.
a. After adjustment for wealth, geographic dimension, and/or stimulation of demand.
b. The first number pertains to the 6-year primary cycle (or whatever the duration of the primary cycle) and the second number to the 9-year primary cycle in ES-5.

GUINEA-BISSAU: Estimated Annual Public Spending on Education and Financing Gap in 2020

2005 US$ million unless otherwise indicated

Policy scenario		Aggregate annual public education spending (recurrent and capital)	Annual recurrent financing gap in **primary or basic education**	Annual recurrent financing gap in **post-primary education** under 3 scenarios for domestic resource mobilization			Annual capital financing gap	Total financing gap as share of total public education spending (%)		
Coverage	Per-student spending at post-primary levels			Scenario 1	Scenario 2	Scenario 3		Scenario 1	Scenario 2	Scenario 3
ES-1	"Generous"	60		26	23	20	7	71	67	62
	"Spartan"	47		14	11	8	6	63	58	52
ES-2	"Generous"	53		19	17	14	6	67	62	57
	"Spartan"	43		10	8	5	6	60	54	47
ES-3	"Generous"	52		18	16	13	6	66	61	56
	"Spartan"	44		11	8	5	5	60	54	48
ES-4	"Generous"	45		13	10	7	5	62	56	50
	"Spartan"	39	10	7	4	1	5	56	49	42
ES-5	"Generous"	43		4	1	−2	7	59	53	46
	"Spartan"	42	15	3	0	−2	7	59	52	46

Notes: Rate of real growth of per capita GDP: 2% per year.

Enrollment scenarios: The five scenarios for coverage or enrollment are described on pages 16–18.

Resource mobilization scenarios: Scenarios 1–3 assume a budget allocation for education of 20%, 23%, and 26%, respectively, see also pages 43–44.

Shaded cells: Dependency on external financing 35% or less.

KENYA

KENYA: Enrollments Under Different Policy Scenarios, Base Year and 2020

		Primary	Lower secondary			Upper secondary			Tertiary
			General	TVET	School-to-work transition program	General	TVET	School-to-work transition program	
	2005	7,320,765				890,822	n/a	n/a	91,541
2020	ES-1	11,227,719				2,350,418	106,670	198,607	257,229
	ES-2	11,227,719				2,350,418	106,670	198,607	257,229
	ES-3	11,227,719				391,154	33,531	995,764	166,960
	ES-4	11,227,719				361,519	16,407	510,717	136,156
	ES-5	11,515,684				265,964	15,806	405,964	136,156

Note: Rate of real growth of per capita GDP: 2% per year.

KENYA: GER and Other Parameters Under Different Policy Scenarios, Base Year and 2020

		Primary GER (%)	Lower secondary GER (%)			Upper secondary GER (%)			Higher education GER (%) and other indicators		
			General	TVET	School-to-work transition program	General	TVET	School-to-work transition program	GER (%)	Students/ 100,000	Unemployment (simulated) (%)
	2005	104.7				27.1	n/a	n/a	3.1	273	n/a
2020	ES-1	108.3				53.9	9.3	16.6	7.1	519	33
	ES-2	108.3				53.9	9.3	16.6	7.1	519	33
	ES-3	108.3				9.0	2.9	83.4	4.6	337	25
	ES-4	108.3				8.3	1.4	42.8	3.7	275	20
	ES-5	100.0				8.3	1.4	35.3	3.7	275	20

Note: Rate of real growth of per capita GDP: 2% per year.

KENYA: Teacher Salaries and Per-Student Spending by Level of Education, Base Year and 2020

		Lower secondary			Upper secondary			Higher education			
	Primary	General	TVET	School-to-work transition program	General	TVET	School-to-work transition program	Humanities & social sciences	Sciences	Professional	All
Teacher salaries in multiples of per capita GDP[a]											
2005	5.3	n/a			10.6						
2020 "Generous"	3.0/3.1[b]	n/a			5.9						
"Spartan"		n/a			5.1						
Level of per-student spending in % of per capita GDP[a]											
2005	16	n/a	140	110	68	140	33	193	221	293	222
2020 "Generous"	13/14[b]	n/a	90	50	55	140	100	151	242	291	200
"Spartan"	n/a	n/a	90	50	29	140	100	151	242	291	200

Note: Rate of real growth of per capita GDP: 2% per year.
a. After adjustment for wealth, geographic dimension, and/or stimulation of demand.
b. The first number pertains to the 6-year primary cycle (or whatever the duration of the primary cycle) and the second number to the 9-year primary cycle in ES-5.

KENYA: Estimated Annual Public Spending on Education and Financing Gap in 2020

2005 US$ million unless otherwise indicated

Policy scenario		Aggregate annual public education spending (recurrent and capital)	Annual recurrent financing gap in **primary or basic education**	Annual recurrent financing gap in **post-primary education** under 3 scenarios for domestic resource mobilization			Annual capital financing gap	Total financing gap as share of total public education spending (%)		
Coverage	Per-student spending at post-primary levels			Scenario 1	Scenario 2	Scenario 3		Scenario 1	Scenario 2	Scenario 3
ES-1	"Generous"	2,115		688	513	337	98	48	39	31
	"Spartan"	1,841		418	243	68	94	40	30	21
ES-2	"Generous"	2,115		688	513	337	98	48	39	31
	"Spartan"	1,841		418	243	68	94	40	30	21
ES-3	"Generous"	1,789		386	211	36	74	38	28	18
	"Spartan"	1,745		341	166	–9	74	36	26	16
ES-4	"Generous"	1,523		120	–55	–230	74	27	16	4
	"Spartan"	1,482	220	79	–97	–272	74	25	13	2
ES-5	"Generous"	1,531		–72	–247	–422	82	28	16	5
	"Spartan"	1,501	412	–102	–277	–452	82	26	14	3

Notes: Rate of real growth of per capita GDP: 2% per year.

Enrollment scenarios: The five scenarios for coverage or enrollment are described on pages 16–18.

Resource mobilization scenarios: Scenarios 1–3 assume a budget allocation for education of 20%, 23%, and 26%, respectively, see also pages 43–44.

Shaded cells: Dependency on external financing 35% or less.

LESOTHO

LESOTHO: Enrollments Under Different Policy Scenarios, Base Year and 2020

| | | | Lower secondary | | | Upper secondary | | | |
		Primary	General	TVET	School-to-work transition program	General	TVET	School-to-work transition program	Tertiary
	2005	427,009	66,109	n/a	n/a	22,009	560	n/a	6,800
2020	ES-1	316,163	103,667	7,680	0	31,341	5,381	4,837	9,829
	ES-2	316,163	78,326	9,216	3,850	23,680	4,066	3,655	7,426
	ES-3	316,163	78,326	9,216	3,850	10,512	3,409	14,054	8,195
	ES-4	316,163	59,896	9,984	6,738	9,097	1,562	5,377	6,257
	ES-5	372,682				13,652	1,564	13,563	6,257

Note: Rate of real growth of per capita GDP: 2% per year.

LESOTHO: GER and Other Parameters Under Different Policy Scenarios, Base Year and 2020

| | | | Lower secondary GER (%) | | | Upper secondary GER (%) | | | Higher education GER (%) and other indicators | | |
		Primary GER (%)	General	TVET	School-to-work transition program	General	TVET	School-to-work transition program	GER (%)	Students/ 100,000	Unemployment (simulated) (%)
	2005	129.6	45.0	n/a	n/a	22.7	0.6	n/a	3.9	379	n/a
2020	ES-1	108.3	85.5	9.5	0.0	38.8	6.7	12.0	6.1	572	28
	ES-2	108.3	64.6	11.4	9.5	29.3	5.0	9.0	4.6	432	23
	ES-3	108.3	64.6	11.4	9.5	13.0	4.2	34.8	5.1	477	25
	ES-4	108.3	49.4	12.4	16.6	11.3	1.9	13.3	3.9	364	20
	ES-5	100.0				11.3	1.9	33.5	3.9	364	20

Note: Rate of real growth of per capita GDP: 2% per year.

LESOTHO: Teacher Salaries and Per-Student Spending by Level of Education, Base Year and 2020

	Primary	Lower secondary			Upper secondary			Higher education			
		General	TVET	School-to-work transition program	General	TVET	School-to-work transition program	Humanities & social sciences	Sciences	Professional	All
Teacher salaries in multiples of per capita GDP[a]											
2005	4.4	9.0			9.0						
2020 "Generous"	3.0/3.1[b]	4.6			5.9						
"Spartan"	4.2	4.2			5.1						
Level of per-student spending in % of per capita GDP[a]											
2005	18	46	140	110	71	160	33	588	671	891	676
2020 "Generous"	13/15[b]	37	90	50	55	140	100	151	242	291	200
"Spartan"	19	19	90	50	29	140	100	151	242	291	200

Note: Rate of real growth of per capita GDP: 2% per year.
a. After adjustment for wealth, geographic dimension, and/or stimulation of demand.
b. The first number pertains to the 6-year primary cycle (or whatever the duration of the primary cycle) and the second number to the 9-year primary cycle in ES-5.

LESOTHO: Estimated Annual Public Spending on Education and Financing Gap in 2020

2005 US$ million unless otherwise indicated

Policy scenario — Coverage	Per-student spending at post-primary levels	Aggregate annual public education spending (recurrent and capital)	Annual recurrent financing gap in **primary or basic education**	Annual recurrent financing gap in **post-primary education** under 3 scenarios for domestic resource mobilization			Annual capital financing gap	Total financing gap as share of total public education spending (%)		
				Scenario 1	Scenario 2	Scenario 3		Scenario 1	Scenario 2	Scenario 3
ES-1	"Generous"	121		57	48	39	1	53	46	38
	"Spartan"	97		32	23	14	1	41	32	23
ES-2	"Generous"	107		42	33	25	1	47	38	30
	"Spartan"	88		24	15	6	0	35	25	15
ES-3	"Generous"	110		46	37	28	1	48	40	32
	"Spartan"	94		30	21	12	0	39	30	20
ES-4	"Generous"	93		30	21	12	0	39	30	20
	"Spartan"	81	7	17	8	–1	0	30	19	8
ES-5	"Generous"	78		6	–3	–12	0	27	16	4
	"Spartan"	76	15	4	–5	–14	0	25	13	1

Notes: Rate of real growth of per capita GDP: 2% per year.
Enrollment scenarios: The five scenarios for coverage or enrollment are described on pages 16–18.
Resource mobilization scenarios: Scenarios 1–3 assume a budget allocation for education of 20%, 23%, and 26%, respectively, see also pages 43–44.
Shaded cells: Dependency on external financing 35% or less.

MADAGASCAR

MADAGASCAR: Enrollments Under Different Policy Scenarios, Base Year and 2020

		Primary	Lower secondary			Upper secondary			Tertiary
			General	TVET	School-to-work transition program	General	TVET	School-to-work transition program	
	2003	3,253,389	344,935	n/a	n/a	68,144	28,680	n/a	36,030
2020	ES-1	3,615,671	2,122,686	178,348	0	680,679	116,873	72,458	530,853
	ES-2	3,615,671	1,603,807	214,017	61,418	514,291	88,304	54,746	401,089
	ES-3	3,615,671	1,603,807	214,017	61,418	136,595	44,301	251,627	73,451
	ES-4	3,615,671	1,226,441	231,852	107,482	132,251	22,708	93,468	62,748
	ES-5	5,820,216				132,251	22,708	215,988	62,748

Note: Rate of real growth of per capita GDP: 2% per year.

MADAGASCAR: GER and Other Parameters Under Different Policy Scenarios, Base Year and 2020

		Primary GER (%)	Lower secondary GER (%)			Upper secondary GER (%)			Higher education GER (%) and other indicators		
			General	TVET	School-to-work transition program	General	TVET	School-to-work transition program	GER (%)	Students/ 100,000	Unemployment (simulated) (%)
	2003	129.7	20.0	n/a	n/a	5.9	2.5	n/a	2.7	199	n/a
2020	ES-1	108.3	85.5	9.5	0.0	38.8	6.7	12.0	25.0	1,997	56
	ES-2	108.3	64.6	11.4	9.5	29.3	5.0	9.0	18.9	1,509	53
	ES-3	108.3	64.6	11.4	9.5	7.8	2.5	41.6	3.5	276	25
	ES-4	108.3	49.4	12.4	16.6	7.5	1.3	15.4	3.0	236	20
	ES-5	100.0				7.5	1.3	35.7	3.0	236	20

Note: Rate of real growth of per capita GDP: 2% per year.

MADAGASCAR: Teacher Salaries and Per-Student Spending by Level of Education, Base Year and 2020

		Lower secondary			Upper secondary			Higher education			
	Primary	General	TVET	School-to-work transition program	General	TVET	School-to-work transition program	Humanities & social sciences	Sciences	Professional	All
Teacher salaries in multiples of per capita GDP[a]											
2003	4.4	4.3			7.7						
2020 "Generous"	3.2/3.4[b]	4.9			6.3						
"Spartan"	4.5				5.5						
Level of per-student spending in % of per capita GDP[a]											
2003	13	27	140	110	73	160	33	193	295	295	234
2020 "Generous"	15/18[b]	43	90	50	65	140	100	187	299	361	248
"Spartan"	21	21	90	50	34	140	100	187	299	361	248

Note: Rate of real growth of per capita GDP: 2% per year.
a. After adjustment for wealth, geographic dimension, and/or stimulation of demand.
b. The first number pertains to the 6-year primary cycle (or whatever the duration of the primary cycle) and the second number to the 9-year primary cycle in ES-5.

MADAGASCAR: Estimated Annual Public Spending on Education and Financing Gap in 2020

2005 US$ million unless otherwise indicated

Policy scenario		Aggregate annual public education spending (recurrent and capital)	Annual recurrent financing gap in **primary or basic education**	Annual recurrent financing gap in **post-primary education** under 3 scenarios for domestic resource mobilization			Annual capital financing gap	Total financing gap as share of total public education spending (%)		
Coverage	Per-student spending at post-primary levels			Scenario 1	Scenario 2	Scenario 3		Scenario 1	Scenario 2	Scenario 3
ES-1	"Generous"	1,358		856	802	748	77	75	71	67
	"Spartan"	1,090		598	544	490	67	69	64	59
ES-2	"Generous"	1,135		645	592	538	63	70	65	61
	"Spartan"	932		450	397	343	56	64	58	52
ES-3	"Generous"	869		385	331	277	58	61	55	49
	"Spartan"	700		223	170	116	51	52	44	36
ES-4	"Generous"	740		264	211	157	50	54	47	40
	"Spartan"	609	87	138	85	31	44	44	35	27
ES-5	"Generous"	663		129	75	22	69	49	41	33
	"Spartan"	651	126	117	64	10	69	48	40	31

Notes: Rate of real growth of per capita GDP: 2% per year.

Enrollment scenarios: The five scenarios for coverage or enrollment are described on pages 16–18.

Resource mobilization scenarios: Scenarios 1–3 assume a budget allocation for education of 20%, 23%, and 26%, respectively, see also pages 43–44 .

Shaded cells: Dependency on external financing 35% or less.

MALAWI

MALAWI: Enrollments Under Different Policy Scenarios, Base Year and 2020

			Lower secondary			Upper secondary			
		Primary	General	TVET	School-to-work transition program	General	TVET	School-to-work transition program	Tertiary
	2002	2,957,596	125,606	n/a	n/a	85,318	n/a	n/a	3,957
2020	ES-1	4,153,310	745,721	82,858	0	328,591	83,936	51,819	17,282
	ES-2	4,153,310	563,434	99,429	42,316	248,269	63,419	39,152	13,058
	ES-3	4,153,310	563,434	99,429	42,316	55,358	26,711	186,977	44,099
	ES-4	4,153,310	430,861	107,715	74,054	55,170	14,093	69,384	38,779
	ES-5	4,273,108				83,401	14,320	159,317	38,779

Note: Rate of real growth of per capita GDP: 2% per year.

MALAWI: GER and Other Parameters Under Different Policy Scenarios, Base Year and 2020

			Lower secondary GER (%)			Upper secondary GER (%)			Higher education GER (%) and other indicators		
		Primary GER (%)	General	TVET	School-to-work transition program	General	TVET	School-to-work transition program	GER (%)	Students/ 100,000	Unemployment (simulated) (%)
	2002	106.2	22.2	n/a	n/a	16.1	n/a	n/a	0.4	31	n/a
2020	ES-1	108.3	85.5	9.5	0.0	38.8	6.7	12.0	1.1	97	<10
	ES-2	108.3	64.6	11.4	9.5	29.3	5.0	9.0	0.8	73	<10
	ES-3	108.3	64.6	11.4	9.5	6.5	2.1	43.2	2.8	248	25
	ES-4	108.3	49.4	12.4	16.6	6.5	1.1	16.0	2.5	218	20
	ES-5	100.0				6.5	1.1	36.3	2.5	218	20

Note: Rate of real growth of per capita GDP: 2% per year.

MALAWI: Teacher Salaries and Per-Student Spending by Level of Education, Base Year and 2020

		Lower secondary			Upper secondary			Higher education			
	Primary	General	TVET	School-to-work transition program	General	TVET	School-to-work transition program	Humanities & social sciences	Sciences	Professional	All
Teacher salaries in multiples of per capita GDP[a]											
2002	4.2	7.7			7.7						
2020 "Generous"	3.6/3.7[b]	5.5			7.1						
"Spartan"		5.0			6.1						
Level of per-student spending in % of per capita GDP[a]											
2002	8	48	355	110	48	355	33	1,108	1,264	1,679	1,274
2020 "Generous"	19/19[b]	54	90	50	84	140	100	258	413	498	341
"Spartan"	27		90	50	43	140	100	258	413	498	341

Note: Rate of real growth of per capita GDP: 2% per year.
a. After adjustment for wealth, geographic dimension, and/or stimulation of demand.
b. The first number pertains to the 6-year primary cycle (or whatever the duration of the primary cycle) and the second number to the 9-year primary cycle in ES-5.

MALAWI: Estimated Annual Public Spending on Education and Financing Gap in 2020

2005 US$ million unless otherwise indicated

Policy scenario		Aggregate annual public education spending (recurrent and capital)	Annual recurrent financing gap in **primary or basic education**	Annual recurrent financing gap in **post-primary education** under 3 scenarios for domestic resource mobilization			Annual capital financing gap	Total financing gap as share of total public education spending (%)		
Coverage	Per-student spending at post-primary levels			Scenario 1	Scenario 2	Scenario 3		Scenario 1	Scenario 2	Scenario 3
ES-1	"Generous"	506		197	174	152	54	72	67	63
	"Spartan"	421		116	93	70	50	66	60	55
ES-2	"Generous"	458		154	131	108	49	69	64	59
	"Spartan"	393		92	70	47	47	63	58	52
ES-3	"Generous"	454		153	130	108	47	68	63	58
	"Spartan"	405		106	83	61	44	64	59	53
ES-4	"Generous"	409		110	87	65	44	65	59	54
	"Spartan"	370	110	73	51	28	42	61	55	49
ES-5	"Generous"	339		13	−9	−32	40	58	51	44
	"Spartan"	333	142	7	−16	−38	40	57	50	43

Notes: Rate of real growth of per capita GDP: 2% per year.

Enrollment scenarios: The five scenarios for coverage or enrollment are described on pages 16–18.

Resource mobilization scenarios: Scenarios 1–3 assume a budget allocation for education of 20%, 23%, and 26%, respectively; see also pages 43–44.

Shaded cells: Dependency on external financing 35% or less.

MALI

MALI: Enrollments Under Different Policy Scenarios, Base Year and 2020

		Primary	Lower secondary			Upper secondary			Tertiary
			General	TVET	School-to-work transition program	General	TVET	School-to-work transition program	
2004		1,634,245	312,004	n/a	n/a	75,955	n/a	n/a	36,109
2020	ES-1	3,808,276	1,326,217	147,357	0	550,779	64,005	60,074	288,547
	ES-2	3,808,276	1,002,031	176,829	51,931	416,144	48,359	45,389	218,013
	ES-3	3,808,276	1,002,031	176,829	51,931	110,471	24,249	208,646	60,866
	ES-4	3,808,276	766,259	191,565	90,879	105,578	12,269	77,784	51,326
	ES-5	5,066,463				105,578	12,269	179,363	51,326

Note: Rate of real growth of per capita GDP: 2% per year.

MALI: GER and Other Parameters Under Different Policy Scenarios, Base Year and 2020

		Primary GER (%)	Lower secondary GER (%)			Upper secondary GER (%)			Higher education GER (%) and other indicators		
			General	TVET	School-to-work transition program	General	TVET	School-to-work transition program	GER (%)	Students/ 100,000	Unemployment (simulated) (%)
2004		71.9	32.2	n/a	n/a	8.7	n/a	n/a	3.6	275	n/a
2020	ES-1	108.3	85.5	9.5	0.0	38.8	6.7	12.0	17.6	1,380	50
	ES-2	108.3	64.6	11.4	9.5	29.3	5.0	9.0	13.3	1,043	47
	ES-3	108.3	64.6	11.4	9.5	7.8	2.5	41.6	3.7	291	25
	ES-4	108.3	49.4	12.4	16.6	7.4	1.3	15.5	3.1	246	20
	ES-5	100.0				7.4	1.3	35.7	3.1	246	20

Note: Rate of real growth of per capita GDP: 2% per year.

MALI: Teacher Salaries and Per-Student Spending by Level of Education, Base Year and 2020

		Lower secondary			Upper secondary			Higher education			
	Primary	General	TVET	School-to-work transition program	General	TVET	School-to-work transition program	Humanities & social sciences	Sciences	Professional	All
Teacher salaries in multiples of per capita GDP[a]											
2004	6.0	6.8			8.3						
2020 "Generous"	3.1/3.2[b]	4.7			6.0						
"Spartan"		4.3			5.2						
Level of per-student spending in % of per capita GDP[a]											
2004	15	26	203	110	117	203	33	139	158	210	160
2020 "Generous"	14/16[b]	40	90	50	61	140	100	186	298	359	246
"Spartan"	20	20	90	50	32	140	100	186	298	359	246

Note: Rate of real growth of per capita GDP: 2% per year.
a. After adjustment for wealth, geographic dimension, and/or stimulation of demand.
b. The first number pertains to the 6-year primary cycle (or whatever the duration of the primary cycle) and the second number to the 9-year primary cycle in ES-5.

MALI: Estimated Annual Public Spending on Education and Financing Gap in 2020
2005 US$ million unless otherwise indicated

Coverage	Policy scenario — Per-student spending at post-primary levels	Aggregate annual public education spending (recurrent and capital)	Annual recurrent financing gap in **primary or basic education**	Annual recurrent financing gap in **post-primary education** under 3 scenarios for domestic resource mobilization			Annual capital financing gap	Total financing gap as share of total public education spending (%)		
				Scenario 1	Scenario 2	Scenario 3		Scenario 1	Scenario 2	Scenario 3
ES-1	"Generous"	1,095		596	547	498	87	72	67	63
	"Spartan"	902		409	360	312	80	66	60	55
ES-2	"Generous"	948		458	409	361	77	68	62	57
	"Spartan"	802		317	268	220	72	62	56	49
ES-3	"Generous"	794		308	260	211	73	61	55	49
	"Spartan"	678		197	148	100	68	55	47	40
ES-4	"Generous"	697		217	168	120	67	56	49	42
	"Spartan"	606	105	130	81	33	64	49	41	33
ES-5	"Generous"	613		68	19	-30	78	50	42	34
	"Spartan"	602	159	57	9	-40	78	49	41	33

Notes: Rate of real growth of per capita GDP: 2% per year.
Enrollment scenarios: The five scenarios for coverage or enrollment are described on pages 16–18.
Resource mobilization scenarios: Scenarios 1–3 assume a budget allocation for education of 20%, 23%, and 26%, respectively, see also pages 43–44.
Shaded cells: Dependency on external financing 35% or less.

MAURITANIA

MAURITANIA: Enrollments Under Different Policy Scenarios, Base Year and 2020

		Primary	Lower secondary General	TVET	School-to-work transition program	Upper secondary General	TVET	School-to-work transition program	Tertiary
2004		464,574	55,514	n/a	n/a	39,143	n/a	n/a	8,541
2020	ES-1	742,098	354,667	29,932	0	109,711	18,838	11,939	27,290
	ES-2	742,098	267,971	35,919	10,412	82,893	14,233	9,020	20,619
	ES-3	742,098	267,971	35,919	10,412	26,675	8,651	39,325	14,663
	ES-4	742,098	204,919	38,912	18,220	24,802	4,258	14,696	12,029
	ES-5	1,000,091				33,559	4,386	35,826	12,029

Note: Rate of real growth of per capita GDP: 2% per year.

MAURITANIA: GER and Other Parameters Under Different Policy Scenarios, Base Year and 2020

		Primary GER (%)	Lower secondary GER (%) General	TVET	School-to-work transition program	Upper secondary GER (%) General	TVET	School-to-work transition program	Higher education GER (%) and other indicators GER (%)	Students/ 100,000	Unemployment (simulated) (%)
2004		100.5	21.2	n/a	n/a	21.9	n/a	n/a	3.9	287	n/a
2020	ES-1	108.3	85.5	9.5	0.0	38.8	6.7	12.0	8.1	610	36
	ES-2	108.3	64.6	11.4	9.5	29.3	5.0	9.0	6.1	461	32
	ES-3	108.3	64.6	11.4	9.5	9.4	3.1	39.4	4.4	328	25
	ES-4	108.3	49.4	12.4	16.6	8.8	1.5	14.7	3.6	269	20
	ES-5	100.0				8.8	1.5	35.0	3.6	269	20

Note: Rate of real growth of per capita GDP: 2% per year.

MAURITANIA: Teacher Salaries and Per-Student Spending by Level of Education, Base Year and 2020

		Lower secondary			Upper secondary			Higher education			
	Primary	General	TVET	School-to-work transition program	General	TVET	School-to-work transition program	Humanities & social sciences	Sciences	Professional	All
Teacher salaries in multiples of per capita GDP[a]											
2004	3.3				4.8						
2020 "Generous"	3.0/3.2[b]	4.6			5.9						
"Spartan"		4.2			5.1						
Level of per-student spending in % of per capita GDP[a]											
2004	11	31	147	110	42	147	33	69	79	105	80
2020 "Generous"	13/15[b]	37	90	50	55	140	100	151	242	291	200
"Spartan"	18	18	90	50	29	140	100	151	242	291	200

Note: Rate of real growth of per capita GDP: 2% per year.
a. After adjustment for wealth, geographic dimension, and/or stimulation of demand.
b. The first number pertains to the 6-year primary cycle (or whatever the duration of the primary cycle) and the second number to the 9-year primary cycle in ES-5.

MAURITANIA: Estimated Annual Public Spending on Education and Financing Gap in 2020

2005 US$ million unless otherwise indicated

Coverage	Policy scenario — Per-student spending at post-primary levels	Aggregate annual public education spending (recurrent and capital)	Annual recurrent financing gap in **primary or basic education**	Annual recurrent financing gap in **post-primary education** under 3 scenarios for domestic resource mobilization			Annual capital financing gap	Total financing gap as share of total public education spending (%)		
				Scenario 1	Scenario 2	Scenario 3		Scenario 1	Scenario 2	Scenario 3
ES-1	"Generous"	244		122	107	92	15	61	54	48
	"Spartan"	189		69	54	39	13	49	41	33
ES-2	"Generous"	212		92	77	62	12	55	48	40
	"Spartan"	170		52	37	22	11	44	35	26
ES-3	"Generous"	203		85	70	55	12	53	45	38
	"Spartan"	168		51	36	21	10	43	34	25
ES-4	"Generous"	174		57	42	27	10	45	36	28
	"Spartan"	147	11	31	16	1	9	35	24	14
ES-5	"Generous"	143		17	2	–13	12	33	22	12
	"Spartan"	139	18	14	–2	–17	11	31	20	9

Notes: Rate of real growth of per capita GDP: 2% per year.

Enrollment scenarios: The five scenarios for coverage or enrollment are described on pages 16–18.

Resource mobilization scenarios: Scenarios 1–3 assume a budget allocation for education of 20%, 23%, and 26%, respectively, see also pages 43–44.

Shaded cells: Dependency on external financing 35% or less.

MOZAMBIQUE

MOZAMBIQUE: Enrollments Under Different Policy Scenarios, Base Year and 2020

| | | | Lower secondary | | | Upper secondary | | | |
		Primary	General	TVET	School-to-work transition program	General	TVET	School-to-work transition program	Tertiary
	2001	2,949,260	167,792	n/a	n/a	26,285	11,550	n/a	15,874
2020	ES-1	4,944,416	1,552,402	115,825	0	452,664	115,622	71,397	303,441
	ES-2	4,944,416	1,172,926	138,990	59,163	342,013	87,359	53,944	229,267
	ES-3	4,944,416	1,172,926	138,990	59,163	84,489	40,763	252,157	67,316
	ES-4	4,944,416	896,944	150,572	103,535	82,773	21,142	93,616	58,190
	ES-5	5,783,286				125,136	21,486	217,512	58,190

Note: Rate of real growth of per capita GDP: 2% per year.

MOZAMBIQUE: GER and Other Parameters Under Different Policy Scenarios, Base Year and 2020

| | | | Lower secondary GER (%) | | | Upper secondary GER (%) | | | Higher education GER (%) and other indicators | | |
		Primary GER (%)	General	TVET	School-to-work transition program	General	TVET	School-to-work transition program	GER (%)	Students/ 100,000	Unemployment (simulated) (%)
	2001	80.4	12.3	n/a	n/a	3.1	0.9	n/a	1.1	82	n/a
2020	ES-1	108.3	85.5	9.5	0.0	38.8	6.7	12.0	14.0	1,189	51
	ES-2	108.3	64.6	11.4	9.5	29.3	5.0	9.0	10.6	899	47
	ES-3	108.3	64.6	11.4	9.5	7.2	2.4	42.3	3.1	264	25
	ES-4	108.3	49.4	12.4	16.6	7.1	1.2	15.7	2.7	228	20
	ES-5	100.0				7.1	1.2	35.9	2.7	228	20

Note: Rate of real growth of per capita GDP: 2% per year.

MOZAMBIQUE: Teacher Salaries and Per-Student Spending by Level of Education, Base Year and 2020

		Lower secondary			Upper secondary			Higher education			
	Primary	General	TVET	School-to-work transition program	General	TVET	School-to-work transition program	Humanities & social sciences	Sciences	Professional	All
Teacher salaries in multiples of per capita GDP[a]											
2001	3.9	9.4			23.8						
2020 "Generous"	3.4/3.5[b]	5.2			6.6						
"Spartan"		4.7			5.7						
Level of per-student spending in % of per capita GDP[a]											
2001	9	32	30	110	138	57	33	489	559	742	563
2020 "Generous"	15/16[b]	42	90	50	65	140	100	166	265	319	219
"Spartan"		21	90	50	34	140	100	166	265	319	219

Note: Rate of real growth of per capita GDP: 2% per year.

a. After adjustment for wealth, geographic dimension, and/or stimulation of demand.

b. The first number pertains to the 6-year primary cycle (or whatever the duration of the primary cycle) and the second number to the 9-year primary cycle in ES-5.

MOZAMBIQUE: Estimated Annual Public Spending on Education and Financing Gap in 2020

2005 US$ million unless otherwise indicated

Policy scenario		Aggregate annual public education spending (recurrent and capital)	Annual recurrent financing gap in **primary or basic education**	Annual recurrent financing gap in **post-primary education** under 3 scenarios for domestic resource mobilization			Annual capital financing gap	Total financing gap as share of total public education spending (%)		
Coverage	Per-student spending at post-primary levels			Scenario 1	Scenario 2	Scenario 3		Scenario 1	Scenario 2	Scenario 3
ES-1	"Generous"	933		487	443	399	69	70	65	61
	"Spartan"	772		333	289	245	63	64	58	53
ES-2	"Generous"	808		371	327	283	61	66	60	55
	"Spartan"	687		255	211	167	56	59	53	47
ES-3	"Generous"	701		267	223	179	58	60	54	48
	"Spartan"	600		170	126	82	53	54	46	39
ES-4	"Generous"	611		182	138	94	52	54	47	40
	"Spartan"	532	98	106	62	18	49	48	39	31
ES-5	"Generous"	511		27	-17	-61	52	45	37	28
	"Spartan"	501	153	18	-26	-70	52	44	36	27

Notes: Rate of real growth of per capita GDP: 2% per year.

Enrollment scenarios: The five scenarios for coverage or enrollment are described on pages 16–18.

Resource mobilization scenarios: Scenarios 1–3 assume a budget allocation for education of 20%, 23%, and 26%, respectively; see also pages 43–44.

Shaded cells: Dependency on external financing 35% or less.

NIGER

NIGER: Enrollments Under Different Policy Scenarios, Base Year and 2020

		Primary	Lower secondary			Upper secondary			Tertiary
			General	TVET	School-to-work transition program	General	TVET	School-to-work transition program	
2002		889,323	121,283	n/a	n/a	21,414	n/a	n/a	6,585
2020	ES-1	4,135,090	1,867,659	157,997	0	570,187	97,902	62,396	226,186
	ES-2	4,135,090	1,411,120	189,597	55,841	430,808	73,970	47,143	170,896
	ES-3	4,135,090	1,411,120	189,597	55,841	102,395	33,209	222,223	56,601
	ES-4	4,135,090	1,079,092	205,397	97,722	101,701	17,462	82,334	49,604
	ES-5	5,480,137				137,813	18,033	193,691	49,604

Note: Rate of real growth of per capita GDP: 2% per year.

NIGER: GER and Other Parameters Under Different Policy Scenarios, Base Year and 2020

		Primary GER (%)	Lower secondary GER (%)			Upper secondary GER (%)			Higher education GER (%) and other indicators		
			General	TVET	School-to-work transition program	General	TVET	School-to-work transition program	GER (%)	Students/ 100,000	Unemployment (simulated) (%)
2002		38.7	9.7	n/a	n/a	2.6	n/a	n/a	0.7	49	n/a
2020	ES-1	108.3	85.5	9.5	0.0	38.8	6.7	12.0	13.1	1,001	50
	ES-2	108.3	64.6	11.4	9.5	29.3	5.0	9.0	9.9	757	47
	ES-3	108.3	64.6	11.4	9.5	7.0	2.3	42.6	3.3	251	25
	ES-4	108.3	49.4	12.4	16.6	6.9	1.2	15.8	2.9	220	20
	ES-5	100.0				6.9	1.2	36.0	2.9	220	20

Note: Rate of real growth of per capita GDP: 2% per year.

NIGER: Teacher Salaries and Per-Student Spending by Level of Education, Base Year and 2020

		Lower secondary			Upper secondary			Higher education			
	Primary	General	TVET	School-to-work transition program	General	TVET	School-to-work transition program	Humanities & social sciences	Sciences	Professional	All
Teacher salaries in multiples of per capita GDP[a]											
2002	5.5	8.5			10.2						
2020 "Generous"	3.6/3.7[b]	5.4			7.0						
"Spartan"	5.0	5.0			6.0						
Level of per-student spending in % of per capita GDP[a]											
2002	20	49	820	110	157	820	33	424	484	643	488
2020 "Generous"	17/20[b]	50	90	50	75	140	100	212	339	409	280
"Spartan"	25	25	90	50	39	140	100	212	339	409	280

Note: Rate of real growth of per capita GDP: 2% per year.

a. After adjustment for wealth, geographic dimension, and/or stimulation of demand.

b. The first number pertains to the 6-year primary cycle (or whatever the duration of the primary cycle) and the second number to the 9-year primary cycle in ES-5.

NIGER: Estimated Annual Public Spending on Education and Financing Gap in 2020
2005 US$ million unless otherwise indicated

Policy scenario		Aggregate annual public education spending (recurrent and capital)	Annual recurrent financing gap in **primary or basic education**	Annual recurrent financing gap in **post-primary education** under 3 scenarios for domestic resource mobilization			Annual capital financing gap	Total financing gap as share of total public education spending (%)		
Coverage	Per-student spending at post-primary levels			Scenario 1	Scenario 2	Scenario 3		Scenario 1	Scenario 2	Scenario 3
ES-1	"Generous"	875		479	448	417	94	78	74	71
	"Spartan"	690		302	271	240	85	72	67	63
ES-2	"Generous"	752		367	336	305	83	74	70	66
	"Spartan"	612		233	202	171	76	68	63	58
ES-3	"Generous"	657		276	245	214	78	70	66	61
	"Spartan"	540		165	134	103	73	64	58	52
ES-4	"Generous"	575		200	169	139	72	66	61	55
	"Spartan"	484	107	114	83	52	67	60	53	47
ES-5	"Generous"	485		52	21	−9	76	60	53	47
	"Spartan"	475	161	43	12	−19	76	59	52	46

Notes: Rate of real growth of per capita GDP: 2% per year.
Enrollment scenarios: The five scenarios for coverage or enrollment are described on pages 16–18.
Resource mobilization scenarios: Scenarios 1–3 assume a budget allocation for education of 20%, 23%, and 26%, respectively, see also pages 43–44.
Shaded cells: Dependency on external financing 35% or less.

NIGERIA

NIGERIA: Enrollments Under Different Policy Scenarios, Base Year and 2020

| | | | Lower secondary | | | Upper secondary | | | |
		Primary	General	TVET	School-to-work transition program	General	TVET	School-to-work transition program	Tertiary
	2005	22,566,255	3,530,518	n/a	n/a	2,717,890	50,350	n/a	1,494,080
2020	ES-1	29,032,374	10,664,552	1,184,950	0	4,588,183	530,240	489,089	2,879,106
	ES-2	29,032,374	8,057,661	1,421,940	408,270	3,466,627	400,626	369,534	2,175,325
	ES-3	29,032,374	8,057,661	1,421,940	408,270	1,438,815	314,082	1,465,991	774,759
	ES-4	29,032,374	6,161,741	1,540,435	714,473	1,261,847	145,827	557,582	599,530
	ES-5	39,272,275				1,261,847	145,827	1,384,580	599,530

Note: Rate of real growth of per capita GDP: 2% per year.

NIGERIA: GER and Other Parameters Under Different Policy Scenarios, Base Year and 2020

| | | | Lower secondary GER (%) | | | Upper secondary GER (%) | | | Higher education GER (%) and other indicators | | |
		Primary GER (%)	General	TVET	School-to-work transition program	General	TVET	School-to-work transition program	GER (%)	Students/ 100,000	Unemployment (simulated) (%)
	2005	106.3	37.2	n/a	n/a	31.3	0.9	n/a	15.1	1,162	n/a
2020	ES-1	108.3	85.5	9.5	0.0	38.8	6.7	12.0	20.1	1,638	44
	ES-2	108.3	64.6	11.4	9.5	29.3	5.0	9.0	15.2	1,237	40
	ES-3	108.3	64.6	11.4	9.5	12.2	4.0	35.9	5.4	441	25
	ES-4	108.3	49.4	12.4	16.6	10.7	1.8	13.6	4.2	341	20
	ES-5	100.0				10.7	1.8	33.9	4.2	341	20

Note: Rate of real growth of per capita GDP: 2% per year.

NIGERIA: Teacher Salaries and Per-Student Spending by Level of Education, Base Year and 2020

		Lower secondary			Upper secondary			Higher education			
	Primary	General	TVET	School-to-work transition program	General	TVET	School-to-work transition program	Humanities & social sciences	Sciences	Professional	All
Teacher salaries in multiples of per capita GDP[a]											
2005	4.9	7.2			7.2						
2020 "Generous"	3.0/3.2[b]	4.6			5.9						
"Spartan"		4.2			5.1						
Level of per-student spending in % of per capita GDP[a]											
2005	14	29	33	110	39	33	33	83	94	125	95
2020 "Generous"	13/15[b]	36	90	50	55	140	100	151	242	291	200
"Spartan"	18	18	90	50	29	140	100	151	242	291	200

Note: Rate of real growth of per capita GDP: 2% per year.

a. After adjustment for wealth, geographic dimension, and/or stimulation of demand.

b. The first number pertains to the 6-year primary cycle (or whatever the duration of the primary cycle) and the second number to the 9-year primary cycle in ES-5.

NIGERIA: Estimated Annual Public Spending on Education and Financing Gap in 2020
2005 US$ million unless otherwise indicated

Policy scenario		Aggregate annual public education spending (recurrent and capital)	Annual recurrent financing gap in **primary or basic education**	Annual recurrent financing gap in **post-primary education** under 3 scenarios for domestic resource mobilization			Annual capital financing gap	Total financing gap as share of total public education spending (%)		
Coverage	Per-student spending at post-primary levels			Scenario 1	Scenario 2	Scenario 3		Scenario 1	Scenario 2	Scenario 3
ES-1	"Generous"	14,884		8,287	7,431	6,575	636	64	58	52
	"Spartan"	12,347		5,810	4,954	4,098	577	56	49	42
ES-2	"Generous"	12,789		6,273	5,417	4,561	556	58	51	44
	"Spartan"	10,873		4,402	3,546	2,690	511	50	42	34
ES-3	"Generous"	10,713		4,223	3,367	2,511	529	49	41	33
	"Spartan"	9,123		2,673	1,817	960	490	41	31	22
ES-4	"Generous"	9,231		2,787	1,931	1,075	483	41	32	23
	"Spartan"	7,991	539	1,576	720	-136	454	32	21	11
ES-5	"Generous"	8,021		1,062	206	-650	599	32	22	11
	"Spartan"	7,822	939	862	6	-850	599	31	20	9

Notes: Rate of real growth of per capita GDP: 2% per year.
Enrollment scenarios: The five scenarios for coverage or enrollment are described on pages 16–18.
Resource mobilization scenarios: Scenarios 1–3 assume a budget allocation for education of 20%, 23%, and 26%, respectively; see also pages 43–44.
Shaded cells: Dependency on external financing 35% or less.

RWANDA

RWANDA: Enrollments Under Different Policy Scenarios, Base Year and 2020

			Lower secondary			Upper secondary			
		Primary	General	TVET	School-to-work transition program	General	TVET	School-to-work transition program	Tertiary
2003		1,649,656	165,729	n/a	n/a	96,755	9,141	n/a	21,696
2020	ES-1	2,078,165	738,745	82,083	0	308,242	52,926	33,514	102,883
	ES-2	2,078,165	558,163	98,499	28,804	232,894	39,988	25,321	77,734
	ES-3	2,078,165	558,163	98,499	28,804	56,468	18,314	118,850	31,013
	ES-4	2,078,165	426,830	106,708	50,408	56,059	9,625	44,005	27,166
	ES-5	2,782,335				56,059	9,625	100,673	27,166

Note: Rate of real growth of per capita GDP: 2% per year.

RWANDA: GER and Other Parameters Under Different Policy Scenarios, Base Year and 2020

		Primary GER (%)	Lower secondary GER (%)			Upper secondary GER (%)			Higher education GER (%) and other indicators		
			General	TVET	School-to-work transition program	General	TVET	School-to-work transition program	GER (%)	Students/ 100,000	Unemployment (simulated) (%)
2003		112.6	23.5	n/a	n/a	14.2	1.3	n/a	2.8	246	n/a
2020	ES-1	108.3	85.5	9.5	0.0	38.8	6.7	12.0	10.9	833	48
	ES-2	108.3	64.6	11.4	9.5	29.3	5.0	9.0	8.2	629	44
	ES-3	108.3	64.6	11.4	9.5	7.1	2.3	42.4	3.3	251	25
	ES-4	108.3	49.4	12.4	16.6	7.1	1.2	15.7	2.9	220	20
	ES-5	100.0				7.1	1.2	36.0	2.9	220	20

Note: Rate of real growth of per capita GDP: 2% per year.

RWANDA: Teacher Salaries and Per-Student Spending by Level of Education, Base Year and 2020

		Lower secondary			Upper secondary			Higher education			
	Primary	General	TVET	School-to-work transition program	General	TVET	School-to-work transition program	Humanities & social sciences	Sciences	Professional	All
Teacher salaries in multiples of per capita GDP[a]											
2003	3.9	5.9			6.4						
2020 "Generous"	3.0/3.2[b]	5.4			7.0						
"Spartan"		5.0			6.0						
Level of per-student spending in % of per capita GDP[a]											
2003	8	51	12	110	63	14	33	588	671	891	676
2020 "Generous"	16/19[b]	47	90	50	71	140	100	185	296	357	245
"Spartan"	23	23	90	50	37	140	100	185	296	357	245

Note: Rate of real growth of per capita GDP: 2% per year.
a. After adjustment for wealth, geographic dimension, and/or stimulation of demand.
b. The first number pertains to the 6-year primary cycle (or whatever the duration of the primary cycle) and the second number to the 9-year primary cycle in ES-5.

RWANDA: Estimated Annual Public Spending on Education and Financing Gap in 2020
2005 US$ million unless otherwise indicated

Policy scenario		Aggregate annual public education spending (recurrent and capital)	Annual recurrent financing gap in **primary or basic education**	Annual recurrent financing gap in **post-primary education** under 3 scenarios for domestic resource mobilization			Annual capital financing gap	Total financing gap as share of total public education spending (%)		
Coverage	Per-student spending at post-primary levels			Scenario 1	Scenario 2	Scenario 3		Scenario 1	Scenario 2	Scenario 3
ES-1	"Generous"	380		193	176	159	34	72	67	63
	"Spartan"	304		121	104	87	31	65	59	53
ES-2	"Generous"	330		148	131	114	29	67	62	57
	"Spartan"	273		93	76	59	27	60	54	48
ES-3	"Generous"	291		112	95	78	27	63	57	51
	"Spartan"	246		69	52	35	24	56	49	42
ES-4	"Generous"	255		79	62	45	24	58	51	44
	"Spartan"	220	44	45	28	11	22	51	43	35
ES-5	"Generous"	228		22	5	-12	29	53	45	38
	"Spartan"	224	68	19	2	-15	29	52	44	37

Notes: Rate of real growth of per capita GDP: 2% per year.
Enrollment scenarios: The five scenarios for coverage or enrollment are described on pages 16–18.
Resource mobilization scenarios: Scenarios 1–3 assume a budget allocation for education of 20%, 23%, and 26%, respectively, see also pages 43–44.
Shaded cells: Dependency on external financing 35% or less.

SENEGAL

SENEGAL: Enrollments Under Different Policy Scenarios, Base Year and 2020

| | | | Lower secondary | | | Upper secondary | | | |
		Primary	General	TVET	School-to-work transition program	General	TVET	School-to-work transition program	Tertiary
	2003	1,271,815	257,993	n/a	n/a	72,371	10,866	n/a	55,100
2020	ES-1	2,477,987	1,225,214	102,931	0	392,700	67,427	41,837	367,750
	ES-2	2,477,987	925,718	123,517	35,273	296,707	50,945	31,610	277,855
	ES-3	2,477,987	925,718	123,517	35,273	115,249	37,378	128,944	62,022
	ES-4	2,477,987	707,902	133,810	61,728	103,457	17,764	48,595	49,127
	ES-5	3,370,858				139,222	18,096	121,373	49,127

Note: Rate of real growth of per capita GDP: 2% per year.

SENEGAL: GER and Other Parameters Under Different Policy Scenarios, Base Year and 2020

| | | | Lower secondary GER (%) | | | Upper secondary GER (%) | | | Higher education GER (%) and other indicators | | |
		Primary GER (%)	General	TVET	School-to-work transition program	General	TVET	School-to-work transition program	GER (%)	Students/ 100,000	Unemployment (simulated) (%)
	2003	68.7	23.0	n/a	n/a	9.4	1.4	n/a	6.1	484	n/a
2020	ES-1	108.3	85.5	9.5	0.0	38.8	6.7	12.0	29.3	2,302	50
	ES-2	108.3	64.6	11.4	9.5	29.3	5.0	9.0	22.1	1,740	47
	ES-3	108.3	64.6	11.4	9.5	11.4	3.7	36.9	4.9	388	25
	ES-4	108.3	49.4	12.4	16.6	10.2	1.8	13.9	3.9	308	20
	ES-5	100.0				10.2	1.8	34.1	3.9	308	20

Note: Rate of real growth of per capita GDP: 2% per year.

SENEGAL: Teacher Salaries and Per-Student Spending by Level of Education, Base Year and 2020

	Primary	Lower secondary			Upper secondary			Higher education			
	General	General	TVET	School-to-work transition program	General	TVET	School-to-work transition program	Humanities & social sciences	Sciences	Professional	All
Teacher salaries in multiples of per capita GDP[a]											
2003	4.6	6.2			7.1						
2020 "Generous"	3.0/3.2[b]	4.6			5.9						
"Spartan"		4.2			5.1						
Level of per-student spending in % of per capita GDP[a]											
2003	15	22	67	110	36	370	33	208	238	316	240
2020 "Generous"	13/15[b]	37	90	50	55	140	100	151	242	291	200
"Spartan"	18	18	90	50	29	140	100	151	242	291	200

Note: Rate of real growth of per capita GDP: 2% per year.

a. After adjustment for wealth, geographic dimension, and/or stimulation of demand.

b. The first number pertains to the 6-year primary cycle (or whatever the duration of the primary cycle) and the second number to the 9-year primary cycle in ES-5.

SENEGAL: Estimated Annual Public Spending on Education and Financing Gap in 2020
2005 US$ million unless otherwise indicated

Policy scenario		Aggregate annual public education spending (recurrent and capital)	Annual recurrent financing gap in **primary or basic education**	Annual recurrent financing gap in **post-primary education** under 3 scenarios for domestic resource mobilization			Annual capital financing gap	Total financing gap as share of total public education spending (%)		
Coverage	Per-student spending at post-primary levels			Scenario 1	Scenario 2	Scenario 3		Scenario 1	Scenario 2	Scenario 3
ES-1	"Generous"	1,347		831	763	694	53	68	63	58
	"Spartan"	1,109		598	530	461	47	61	55	49
ES-2	"Generous"	1,135		626	558	490	45	62	56	50
	"Spartan"	955		450	382	314	41	55	48	40
ES-3	"Generous"	893		386	318	250	43	52	44	36
	"Spartan"	738		236	167	99	39	41	32	23
ES-4	"Generous"	759		257	189	121	38	43	34	25
	"Spartan"	638	31	140	72	3	35	32	22	11
ES-5	"Generous"	624		90	22	-47	43	31	20	9
	"Spartan"	604	59	71	2	-66	43	28	17	6

Notes: Rate of real growth of per capita GDP: 2% per year.
Enrollment scenarios: The five scenarios for coverage or enrollment are described on pages 16–18.
Resource mobilization scenarios: Scenarios 1–3 assume a budget allocation for education of 20%, 23%, and 26%, respectively, see also pages 43–44.
Shaded cells: Dependency on external financing 35% or less.

SIERRA LEONE

SIERRA LEONE: Enrollments Under Different Policy Scenarios, Base Year and 2020

			Lower secondary			Upper secondary			
		Primary	General	TVET	School-to-work transition program	General	TVET	School-to-work transition program	Tertiary
	2004	1,191,556	140,071	n/a	n/a	38,707	n/a	n/a	13,693
2020	ES-1	1,301,934	458,427	50,936	0	191,114	32,814	20,788	68,284
	ES-2	1,301,934	346,367	61,124	17,867	144,397	24,793	15,706	51,593
	ES-3	1,301,934	346,367	61,124	17,867	34,477	11,182	73,963	18,943
	ES-4	1,301,934	264,869	66,217	31,268	34,467	5,918	27,353	16,710
	ES-5	1,737,957				34,467	5,918	62,503	16,710

Note: Rate of real growth of per capita GDP: 2% per year.

SIERRA LEONE: GER and Other Parameters Under Different Policy Scenarios, Base Year and 2020

			Lower secondary GER (%)			Upper secondary GER (%)			Higher education GER (%) and other indicators		
		Primary GER (%)	General	TVET	School-to-work transition program	General	TVET	School-to-work transition program	GER (%)	Students/ 100,000	Unemployment (simulated) (%)
	2004	149.8	39.7	n/a	n/a	12.0	n/a	n/a	3.7	258	n/a
2020	ES-1	108.3	85.5	9.5	0.0	38.8	6.7	12.0	11.9	882	49
	ES-2	108.3	64.6	11.4	9.5	29.3	5.0	9.0	9.0	666	45
	ES-3	108.3	64.6	11.4	9.5	7.0	2.3	42.6	3.3	245	25
	ES-4	108.3	49.4	12.4	16.6	7.0	1.2	15.8	2.9	216	20
	ES-5	100.0				7.0	1.2	36.0	2.9	216	20

Note: Rate of real growth of per capita GDP: 2% per year.

SIERRA LEONE: Teacher Salaries and Per-Student Spending by Level of Education, Base Year and 2020

		Lower secondary			Upper secondary			Higher education			
	Primary	General	TVET	School-to-work transition program	General	TVET	School-to-work transition program	Humanities & social sciences	Sciences	Professional	All
Teacher salaries in multiples of per capita GDP[a]											
2004	4.2	5.9			5.9						
2020 "Generous"	3.6/3.8[b]	5.6			7.2						
"Spartan"	5.1				6.2						
Level of per-student spending in % of per capita GDP[a]											
2004	10	29	73	110	30	73	33	253	289	383	291
2020 "Generous"	18/21[b]	54	90	50	85	140	100	255	408	493	338
"Spartan"	26		90	50	43	140	100	255	408	493	338

Note: Rate of real growth of per capita GDP: 2% per year.
a. After adjustment for wealth, geographic dimension, and/or stimulation of demand.
b. The first number pertains to the 6-year primary cycle (or whatever the duration of the primary cycle) and the second number to the 9-year primary cycle in ES-5.

SIERRA LEONE: Estimated Annual Public Spending on Education and Financing Gap in 2020
2005 US$ million unless otherwise indicated

Policy scenario		Aggregate annual public education spending (recurrent and capital)	Annual recurrent financing gap in **primary or basic education**	Annual recurrent financing gap in **post-primary education** under 3 scenarios for domestic resource mobilization			Annual capital financing gap	Total financing gap as share of total public education spending (%)		
Coverage	Per-student spending at post-primary levels			Scenario 1	Scenario 2	Scenario 3		Scenario 1	Scenario 2	Scenario 3
ES-1	"Generous"	237		129	120	110	20	75	71	68
	"Spartan"	189		83	74	65	18	69	64	59
ES-2	"Generous"	203		98	89	80	17	71	67	62
	"Spartan"	167		64	55	45	15	65	60	54
ES-3	"Generous"	172		69	60	51	15	66	61	55
	"Spartan"	144		42	33	24	14	60	53	47
ES-4	"Generous"	151		50	41	31	14	61	55	49
	"Spartan"	129	29	29	20	10	12	55	48	40
ES-5	"Generous"	138		15	6	-3	19	58	51	44
	"Spartan"	135	45	13	4	-6	19	57	50	43

Notes: Rate of real growth of per capita GDP: 2% per year.
Enrollment scenarios: The five scenarios for coverage or enrollment are described on pages 16–18.
Resource mobilization scenarios: Scenarios 1–3 assume a budget allocation for education of 20%, 23%, and 26%, respectively; see also pages 43–44.
Shaded cells: Dependency on external financing 35% or less.

SUDAN

SUDAN: Enrollments Under Different Policy Scenarios, Base Year and 2020

| | | | Lower secondary | | | Upper secondary | | | |
		Primary	General	TVET	School-to-work transition program	General	TVET	School-to-work transition program	Tertiary
	2003	3,852,981				480,759	n/a	n/a	366,841
2020	ES-1	9,011,209				1,622,911	278,656	169,485	1,399,342
	ES-2	9,011,209				1,622,911	278,656	169,485	1,399,342
	ES-3	9,011,209				317,617	103,011	828,856	167,554
	ES-4	9,011,209				290,734	49,919	427,856	135,328
	ES-5	9,329,777				192,960	49,437	348,735	135,328

Note: Rate of real growth of per capita GDP: 2% per year.

SUDAN: GER and Other Parameters Under Different Policy Scenarios, Base Year and 2020

| | | Primary GER (%) | Lower secondary GER (%) | | | Upper secondary GER (%) | | | Higher education GER (%) and other indicators | | |
			General	TVET	School-to-work transition program	General	TVET	School-to-work transition program	GER (%)	Students/ 100,000	Unemployment (simulated) (%)
	2003	55.3				20.7	n/a	n/a	13.3	1,032	n/a
2020	ES-1	108.3				53.9	9.3	16.6	37.5	2,944	55
	ES-2	108.3				53.9	9.3	16.6	37.5	2,944	55
	ES-3	108.3				10.6	3.4	81.3	4.5	352	25
	ES-4	108.3				9.7	1.7	42.0	3.6	285	20
	ES-5	100.0				9.7	1.7	34.5	3.6	285	20

Note: Rate of real growth of per capita GDP: 2% per year.

SUDAN: Teacher Salaries and Per-Student Spending by Level of Education, Base Year and 2020

		Lower secondary			Upper secondary			Higher education			
	Primary	General	TVET	School-to-work transition program	General	TVET	School-to-work transition program	Humanities & social sciences	Sciences	Professional	All
Teacher salaries in multiples of per capita GDP[a]											
2003	2.2	n/a			3.4						
2020 "Generous"	3.0/3.1[b]	n/a			5.9						
"Spartan"		n/a			5.1						
Level of per-student spending in % of per capita GDP[a]											
2003	8	n/a	33	110	18	33	33	82	93	124	94
2020 "Generous"	12/13[b]	n/a	90	50	55	140	100	151	242	291	200
"Spartan"		n/a	90	50	29	140	100	151	242	291	200

Note: Rate of real growth of per capita GDP: 2% per year.

a. After adjustment for wealth, geographic dimension, and/or stimulation of demand.

b. The first number pertains to the 6-year primary cycle (or whatever the duration of the primary cycle) and the second number to the 9-year primary cycle in ES-5.

SUDAN: Estimated Annual Public Spending on Education and Financing Gap in 2020
2005 US$ million unless otherwise indicated

Policy scenario		Aggregate annual public education spending (recurrent and capital)	Annual recurrent financing gap in **primary or basic education**	Annual recurrent financing gap in **post-primary education** under 3 scenarios for domestic resource mobilization			Annual capital financing gap	Total financing gap as share of total public education spending (%)		
Coverage	Per-student spending at post-primary levels			Scenario 1	Scenario 2	Scenario 3		Scenario 1	Scenario 2	Scenario 3
ES-1	"Generous"	2,982		1,753	1,573	1,394	97	62	56	50
	"Spartan"	2,781		1,554	1,374	1,194	94	59	53	46
ES-2	"Generous"	2,982		1,753	1,573	1,394	97	62	56	50
	"Spartan"	2,781		1,554	1,374	1,194	94	59	53	46
ES-3	"Generous"	1,618		407	227	48	78	30	19	7
	"Spartan"	1,579		368	188	9	78	28	17	5
ES-4	"Generous"	1,332		121	-58	-238	78	15	1	-12
	"Spartan"	1,297	-5	86	-94	-274	78	12	-2	-15
ES-5	"Generous"	1,340		-67	-246	-426	85	15	2	-12
	"Spartan"	1,317	184	-90	-270	-450	85	14	0	-14

Notes: Rate of real growth of per capita GDP: 2% per year.
Enrollment scenarios: The five scenarios for coverage or enrollment are described on pages 16–18.
Resource mobilization scenarios: Scenarios 1–3 assume a budget allocation for education of 20%, 23%, and 26%, respectively; see also pages 43–44.
Shaded cells: Dependency on external financing 35% or less.

TANZANIA

TANZANIA: Enrollments Under Different Policy Scenarios, Base Year and 2020

		Primary	Lower secondary			Upper secondary			Tertiary
			General	TVET	School-to-work transition program	General	TVET	School-to-work transition program	
2002		7,082,355	329,280	n/a	n/a	24,890	n/a	n/a	31,049
2020	ES-1	8,936,792	3,838,086	215,187	0	844,435	144,990	132,421	1,521,120
	ES-2	8,936,792	2,899,887	258,224	108,945	638,018	109,548	100,051	1,149,291
	ES-3	8,936,792	2,899,887	258,224	108,945	175,815	57,021	455,662	139,270
	ES-4	8,936,792	2,217,561	279,743	190,654	169,246	29,060	169,310	118,294
	ES-5	10,514,471				342,366	29,725	400,906	118,294

Note: Rate of real growth of per capita GDP: 2% per year.

TANZANIA: GER and Other Parameters Under Different Policy Scenarios, Base Year and 2020

		Primary GER (%)	Lower secondary GER (%)			Upper secondary GER (%)			Higher education GER (%) and other indicators		
			General	TVET	School-to-work transition program	General	TVET	School-to-work transition program	GER (%)	Students/ 100,000	Unemployment (simulated) (%)
2002		100.4	9.2	n/a	n/a	1.5	n/a	n/a	1.0	83	n/a
2020	ES-1	108.3	85.5	9.5	0.0	38.8	6.7	12.0	36.7	3,088	61
	ES-2	108.3	64.6	11.4	9.5	29.3	5.0	9.0	27.7	2,333	57
	ES-3	108.3	64.6	11.4	9.5	8.1	2.6	41.2	3.4	283	25
	ES-4	108.3	49.4	12.4	16.6	7.8	1.3	15.3	2.9	240	20
	ES-5	100.0				7.8	1.3	35.5	2.9	240	20

Note: Rate of real growth of per capita GDP: 2% per year.

TANZANIA: Teacher Salaries and Per-Student Spending by Level of Education, Base Year and 2020

		Lower secondary			Upper secondary			Higher education			
	Primary	General	TVET	School-to-work transition program	General	TVET	School-to-work transition program	Humanities & social sciences	Sciences	Professional	All
Teacher salaries in multiples of per capita GDP[a]											
2002	3.8	5.2			5.2						
2020 "Generous"	3.1/3.2[b]	4.8			6.2						
"Spartan"	4.4	4.4			5.3						
Level of per-student spending in % of per capita GDP[a]											
2002	12	44	140	110	44	160	33	394	450	597	453
2020 "Generous"	14/16[b]	41	90	50	61	140	100	171	274	330	226
"Spartan"	20	20	90	50	32	140	100	171	274	330	226

Note: Rate of real growth of per capita GDP: 2% per year.

a. After adjustment for wealth, geographic dimension, and/or stimulation of demand.

b. The first number pertains to the 6-year primary cycle (or whatever the duration of the primary cycle) and the second number to the 9-year primary cycle in ES-5.

TANZANIA: Estimated Annual Public Spending on Education and Financing Gap in 2020

2005 US$ million unless otherwise indicated

| Policy scenario | | Aggregate annual public education spending (recurrent and capital) | Annual recurrent financing gap in **primary or basic education** | Annual recurrent financing gap in **post-primary education** under 3 scenarios for domestic resource mobilization | | | Annual capital financing gap | Total financing gap as share of total public education spending (%) | | |
Coverage	Per-student spending at post-primary levels			Scenario 1	Scenario 2	Scenario 3		Scenario 1	Scenario 2	Scenario 3
ES-1	"Generous"	2,907		1,929	1,823	1,717	126	77	73	70
	"Spartan"	2,455		1,495	1,388	1,282	109	73	68	64
ES-2	"Generous"	2,418		1,462	1,356	1,250	104	72	68	63
	"Spartan"	2,077		1,133	1,027	921	91	68	63	57
ES-3	"Generous"	1,680		730	624	518	98	60	54	47
	"Spartan"	1,381		443	337	231	86	51	44	36
ES-4	"Generous"	1,444		508	402	296	84	53	46	39
	"Spartan"	1,212	180	285	179	73	75	45	36	27
ES-5	"Generous"	1,123		74	−32	−138	75	40	31	21
	"Spartan"	1,092	301	44	−63	−169	75	38	29	19

Notes: Rate of real growth of per capita GDP: 2% per year.

Enrollment scenarios: The five scenarios for coverage or enrollment are described on pages 16–18.

Resource mobilization scenarios: Scenarios 1–3 assume a budget allocation for education of 20%, 23%, and 26%, respectively; see also pages 43–44.

Shaded cells: Dependency on external financing 35% or less.

TOGO

TOGO: Enrollments Under Different Policy Scenarios, Base Year and 2020

		Primary	Lower secondary			Upper secondary			Tertiary
			General	TVET	School-to-work transition program	General	TVET	School-to-work transition program	
	2005	774,154	291,804	n/a	n/a	50,650	13,171	n/a	28,236
2020	ES-1	1,401,969	688,727	57,876	0	220,044	37,782	23,498	149,004
	ES-2	1,401,969	520,371	69,451	19,874	166,255	28,546	17,754	112,580
	ES-3	1,401,969	520,371	69,451	19,874	44,521	14,439	81,438	24,016
	ES-4	1,401,969	397,931	75,239	34,779	43,153	7,409	30,232	20,539
	ES-5	1,903,347				58,106	7,558	71,205	20,539

Note: Rate of real growth of per capita GDP: 2% per year.

TOGO: GER and Other Parameters Under Different Policy Scenarios, Base Year and 2020

		Primary GER (%)	Lower secondary GER (%)			Upper secondary GER (%)			Higher education GER (%) and other indicators		
			General	TVET	School-to-work transition program	General	TVET	School-to-work transition program	GER (%)	Students/ 100,000	Unemployment (simulated) (%)
	2005	79.7	51.1	n/a	n/a	13.0	3.4	n/a	6.1	472	n/a
2020	ES-1	108.3	85.5	9.5	0.0	38.8	6.7	12.0	21.4	1,707	54
	ES-2	108.3	64.6	11.4	9.5	29.3	5.0	9.0	16.1	1,289	51
	ES-3	108.3	64.6	11.4	9.5	7.9	2.5	41.5	3.4	275	25
	ES-4	108.3	49.4	12.4	16.6	7.6	1.3	15.4	2.9	235	20
	ES-5	100.0				7.6	1.3	35.6	2.9	235	20

Note: Rate of real growth of per capita GDP: 2% per year.

TOGO: Teacher Salaries and Per-Student Spending by Level of Education, Base Year and 2020

		Lower secondary			Upper secondary			Higher education			
	Primary	General	TVET	School-to-work transition program	General	TVET	School-to-work transition program	Humanities & social sciences	Sciences	Professional	All
Teacher salaries in multiples of per capita GDP[a]											
2005	6.2	8.7			9.0						
2020 "Generous"	3.2/3.4[b]	4.9			6.3						
"Spartan"	4.5				5.5						
Level of per-student spending in % of per capita GDP[a]											
2005	21	19	28	110	32	120	33	132	198	238	168
2020 "Generous"	14/16[b]	40	90	50	62	140	100	166	265	319	219
"Spartan"	20	20	90	50	33	140	100	166	265	319	219

Note: Rate of real growth of per capita GDP: 2% per year.
a. After adjustment for wealth, geographic dimension, and/or stimulation of demand.
b. The first number pertains to the 6-year primary cycle (or whatever the duration of the primary cycle) and the second number to the 9-year primary cycle in ES-5.

TOGO: Estimated Annual Public Spending on Education and Financing Gap in 2020
2005 US$ million unless otherwise indicated

Policy scenario		Aggregate annual public education spending (recurrent and capital)	Annual recurrent financing gap in **primary or basic education**	Annual recurrent financing gap in **post-primary education** under 3 scenarios for domestic resource mobilization			Annual capital financing gap	Total financing gap as share of total public education spending (%)		
Coverage	Per-student spending at post-primary levels			Scenario 1	Scenario 2	Scenario 3		Scenario 1	Scenario 2	Scenario 3
ES-1	"Generous"	405		238	221	203	30	73	69	64
	"Spartan"	323		160	143	126	26	66	61	55
ES-2	"Generous"	343		182	164	147	25	68	63	58
	"Spartan"	282		123	106	88	22	61	55	49
ES-3	"Generous"	284		124	107	90	23	61	55	49
	"Spartan"	233		76	58	41	20	53	45	38
ES-4	"Generous"	244		87	70	53	20	55	48	41
	"Spartan"	204	27	49	32	15	18	46	38	29
ES-5	"Generous"	202		25	8	–10	24	46	37	28
	"Spartan"	197	43	20	3	–14	24	44	35	27

Notes: Rate of real growth of per capita GDP: 2% per year.
Enrollment scenarios: The five scenarios for coverage or enrollment are described on pages 16–18.
Resource mobilization scenarios: Scenarios 1–3 assume a budget allocation for education of 20%, 23%, and 26%, respectively, see also pages 43–44.
Shaded cells: Dependency on external financing 35% or less.

UGANDA

UGANDA: Enrollments Under Different Policy Scenarios, Base Year and 2020

		Primary	Lower secondary			Upper secondary			Tertiary
			General	TVET	School-to-work transition program	General	TVET	School-to-work transition program	
	2002	7,390,881	719,900	16,000	16,000	79,774	n/a	n/a	78,500
2020	ES-1	11,411,202	4,043,596	234,883	0	800,237	70,253	131,984	1,122,121
	ES-2	11,411,202	3,055,162	281,860	125,582	604,623	53,080	99,721	847,825
	ES-3	11,411,202	3,055,162	281,860	125,582	161,674	26,810	457,588	134,697
	ES-4	11,411,202	2,336,300	305,348	219,768	158,004	13,871	169,481	116,153
	ES-5	13,005,873				331,086	15,199	430,250	116,153

Note: Rate of real growth of per capita GDP: 2% per year.

UGANDA: GER and Other Parameters Under Different Policy Scenarios, Base Year and 2020

		Primary GER (%)	Lower secondary GER (%)			Upper secondary GER (%)			Higher education GER (%) and other indicators		
			General	TVET	School-to-work transition program	General	TVET	School-to-work transition program	GER (%)	Students/ 100,000	Unemployment (simulated) (%)
	2002	129.8	27.4	1.2	2.2	6.8	n/a	n/a	3.7	282	n/a
2020	ES-1	108.3	85.5	9.5	0.0	38.8	6.7	12.0	31.0	2,219	59
	ES-2	108.3	64.6	11.4	9.5	29.3	5.0	9.0	23.4	1,677	55
	ES-3	108.3	64.6	11.4	9.5	7.8	2.5	41.5	3.7	266	25
	ES-4	108.3	49.4	12.4	16.6	7.7	1.3	15.4	3.2	230	20
	ES-5	100.0				7.7	1.3	35.6	3.2	230	20

Note: Rate of real growth of per capita GDP: 2% per year.

UGANDA: Teacher Salaries and Per-Student Spending by Level of Education, Base Year and 2020

		Lower secondary			Upper secondary			Higher education			
	Primary	General	TVET	School-to-work transition program	General	TVET	School-to-work transition program	Humanities & social sciences	Sciences	Professional	All
Teacher salaries in multiples of per capita GDP[a]											
2002	3.2	7.4			7.4						
2020 "Generous"	3.3/3.4[b]	5.1			6.6						
"Spartan"		4.7			5.7						
Level of per-student spending in % of per capita GDP[a]											
2002	8	145	108	110	145	108	33	139	159	211	160
2020 "Generous"	15/16[b]	42	90	50	62	140	100	155	247	298	204
"Spartan"	21	21	90	50	33	140	100	155	247	298	204

Note: Rate of real growth of per capita GDP: 2% per year.
a. After adjustment for wealth, geographic dimension, and/or stimulation of demand.
b. The first number pertains to the 6-year primary cycle (or whatever the duration of the primary cycle) and the second number to the 9-year primary cycle in ES-5.

UGANDA: **Estimated Annual Public Spending on Education and Financing Gap in 2020**
2005 US$ million unless otherwise indicated

Policy scenario		Aggregate annual public education spending (recurrent and capital)	Annual recurrent financing gap in **primary or basic education**	Annual recurrent financing gap in **post-primary education** under 3 scenarios for domestic resource mobilization			Annual capital financing gap	Total financing gap as share of total public education spending (%)		
Coverage	Per-student spending at post-primary levels			Scenario 1	Scenario 2	Scenario 3		Scenario 1	Scenario 2	Scenario 3
ES-1	"Generous"	2,304		1,227	1,137	1,046	195	75	71	67
	"Spartan"	1,902		842	752	662	178	70	65	60
ES-2	"Generous"	1,990		936	845	755	173	71	67	62
	"Spartan"	1,686		645	555	465	160	66	61	55
ES-3	"Generous"	1,673		625	535	445	167	66	60	55
	"Spartan"	1,404		368	277	187	154	59	53	46
ES-4	"Generous"	1,480		446	355	265	152	61	55	49
	"Spartan"	1,271	310	246	156	66	143	55	48	41
ES-5	"Generous"	1,189		47	-43	-133	141	52	44	37
	"Spartan"	1,164	429	22	-68	-158	141	51	43	35

Notes: Rate of real growth of per capita GDP: 2% per year.
Enrollment scenarios: The five scenarios for coverage or enrollment are described on pages 16–18.
Resource mobilization scenarios: Scenarios 1–3 assume a budget allocation for education of 20%, 23%, and 26%, respectively; see also pages 43–44.
Shaded cells: Dependency on external financing 35% or less.

ZAMBIA

ZAMBIA: Enrollments Under Different Policy Scenarios, Base Year and 2020

| | | | Lower secondary | | | Upper secondary | | | |
| | | | General | TVET | School-to-work transition program | General | TVET | School-to-work transition program | Tertiary |
		Primary							
	2005	2,194,384	281,771	n/a	n/a	181,622	6,932	n/a	24,553
2020	ES-1	3,081,232	634,219	104,804	0	413,783	71,047	44,021	59,071
	ES-2	3,081,232	479,188	125,765	36,193	312,636	53,680	33,261	44,631
	ES-3	3,081,232	479,188	125,765	36,193	104,042	33,743	143,466	55,913
	ES-4	3,081,232	366,438	136,245	63,338	94,316	16,194	54,036	44,723
	ES-5	3,585,991				94,316	16,194	128,471	44,723

Note: Rate of real growth of per capita GDP: 2% per year.

ZAMBIA: GER and Other Parameters Under Different Policy Scenarios, Base Year and 2020

| | | | Lower secondary GER (%) | | | Upper secondary GER (%) | | | Higher education GER (%) and other indicators | | |
		Primary GER (%)	General	TVET	School-to-work transition program	General	TVET	School-to-work transition program	GER (%)	Students/ 100,000	Unemployment (simulated) (%)
	2005	96.0	48.0	n/a	n/a	22.2	0.8	n/a	2.6	214	n/a
2020	ES-1	108.3	85.5	9.5	0.0	38.8	6.7	12.0	4.5	390	26
	ES-2	108.3	64.6	11.4	9.5	29.3	5.0	9.0	3.4	295	20
	ES-3	108.3	64.6	11.4	9.5	9.8	3.2	39.0	4.3	370	25
	ES-4	108.3	49.4	12.4	16.6	8.9	1.5	14.7	3.4	296	20
	ES-5	100.0				8.9	1.5	34.9	3.4	296	20

Note: Rate of real growth of per capita GDP: 2% per year.

ZAMBIA: Teacher Salaries and Per-Student Spending by Level of Education, Base Year and 2020

	Primary	Lower secondary			Upper secondary			Higher education			
		General	TVET	School-to-work transition program	General	TVET	School-to-work transition program	Humanities & social sciences	Sciences	Professional	All
Teacher salaries in multiples of per capita GDP[a]											
2005	3.1	3.7			4.7						
2020 "Generous"	3.0/3.1[b]	4.6			5.9						
"Spartan"		4.2			5.1						
Level of per-student spending in % of per capita GDP[a]											
2005	8	17	170	110	25	170	33	216	247	328	249
2020 "Generous"	14/15[b]	40	90	50	61	140	100	191	306	369	253
"Spartan"		20	90	50	32	140	100	191	306	369	253

Note: Rate of real growth of per capita GDP: 2% per year.
a. After adjustment for wealth, geographic dimension, and/or stimulation of demand.
b. The first number pertains to the 6-year primary cycle (or whatever the duration of the primary cycle) and the second number to the 9-year primary cycle in ES-5.

ZAMBIA: Estimated Annual Public Spending on Education and Financing Gap in 2020
2005 US$ million unless otherwise indicated

Coverage	Policy scenario — Per-student spending at post-primary levels	Aggregate annual public education spending (recurrent and capital)	Annual recurrent financing gap in **primary or basic education**	Annual recurrent financing gap in **post-primary education** under 3 scenarios for domestic resource mobilization			Annual capital financing gap	Total financing gap as share of total public education spending (%)		
				Scenario 1	Scenario 2	Scenario 3		Scenario 1	Scenario 2	Scenario 3
ES-1	"Generous"	935		438	385	331	42	64	58	53
	"Spartan"	774		281	228	174	38	56	50	43
ES-2	"Generous"	838		346	293	239	36	60	53	47
	"Spartan"	716		227	174	121	34	53	45	38
ES-3	"Generous"	820		330	277	224	34	59	52	46
	"Spartan"	729		242	189	135	32	54	46	39
ES-4	"Generous"	719		232	178	125	31	53	46	38
	"Spartan"	647	118	162	109	56	30	48	40	31
ES-5	"Generous"	622		60	7	-46	40	46	37	29
	"Spartan"	609	185	47	-7	-60	40	45	36	27

Notes: Rate of real growth of per capita GDP: 2% per year.
Enrollment scenarios: The five scenarios for coverage or enrollment are described on pages 16–18.
Resource mobilization scenarios: Scenarios 1–3 assume a budget allocation for education of 20%, 23%, and 26%, respectively; see also pages 43–44.
Shaded cells: Dependency on external financing 35% or less.

ZIMBABWE

ZIMBABWE: Enrollments Under Different Policy Scenarios, Base Year and 2020

| | | | Lower secondary | | | Upper secondary | | | |
		Primary	General	TVET	School-to-work transition program	General	TVET	School-to-work transition program	Tertiary
2003		2,265,360	712,646	10,000	10,000	38,023	n/a	1,045	76,000
2020	ES-1	2,536,623	1,088,474	60,715	0	245,091	63,113	37,876	538,663
	ES-2	2,536,623	822,402	72,857	30,643	185,180	47,685	28,617	406,990
	ES-3	2,536,623	822,402	72,857	30,643	74,730	36,349	114,913	58,337
	ES-4	2,536,623	628,896	78,929	53,626	66,323	17,079	43,490	45,683
	ES-5	2,980,598				132,957	17,138	108,368	45,683

Note: Rate of real growth of per capita GDP: 2% per year.

ZIMBABWE: GER and Other Parameters Under Different Policy Scenarios, Base Year and 2020

| | | | Lower secondary GER (%) | | | Upper secondary GER (%) | | | Higher education GER (%) and other indicators | | |
		Primary GER (%)	General	TVET	School-to-work transition program	General	TVET	School-to-work transition program	GER (%)	Students/ 100,000	Unemployment (simulated) (%)
2003		92.6	51.3	1.4	2.8	5.7	n/a	0.3	6.2	588	n/a
2020	ES-1	108.3	85.5	9.5	0.0	38.8	6.7	12.0	42.6	3,808	55
	ES-2	108.3	64.6	11.4	9.5	29.3	5.0	9.0	32.2	2,877	52
	ES-3	108.3	64.6	11.4	9.5	11.8	3.8	36.3	4.6	412	25
	ES-4	108.3	49.4	12.4	16.6	10.5	1.8	13.7	3.6	323	20
	ES-5	100.0				10.5	1.8	34.0	3.6	323	20

Note: Rate of real growth of per capita GDP: 2% per year.

ZIMBABWE: Teacher Salaries and Per-Student Spending by Level of Education, Base Year and 2020

			Lower secondary			Upper secondary			Higher education			
		Primary	General	TVET	School-to-work transition program	General	TVET	School-to-work transition program	Humanities & social sciences	Sciences	Professional	All
Teacher salaries in multiples of per capita GDP[a]												
	2003	4.1	4.1			4.1						
2020	"Generous"	3.0/3.1[b]	4.6			5.9						
	"Spartan"		4.2			5.1						
Level of per-student spending in % of per capita GDP[a]												
	2003	13	23	140	110	23	160	33	171	195	259	197
2020	"Generous"	13/14[b]	37	90	50	55	140	100	151	242	291	200
	"Spartan"		19	90	50	29	140	100	151	242	291	200

Note: Rate of real growth of per capita GDP: 2% per year.
a. After adjustment for wealth, geographic dimension, and/or stimulation of demand.
b. The first number pertains to the 6-year primary cycle (or whatever the duration of the primary cycle) and the second number to the 9-year primary cycle in ES-5.

ZIMBABWE: Estimated Annual Public Spending on Education and Financing Gap in 2020

2005 US$ million unless otherwise indicated

Coverage	Per-student spending at post-primary levels	Aggregate annual public education spending (recurrent and capital)	Annual recurrent financing gap in **primary or basic education**	Annual recurrent financing gap in **post-primary education** under 3 scenarios for domestic resource mobilization			Annual capital financing gap	Total financing gap as share of total public education spending (%)		
				Scenario 1	Scenario 2	Scenario 3		Scenario 1	Scenario 2	Scenario 3
ES-1	"Generous"	1,642		1,160	1,087	1,014	19	72	68	63
	"Spartan"	1,430		952	880	807	14	68	63	58
ES-2	"Generous"	1,344		868	796	723	12	66	60	55
	"Spartan"	1,184		712	639	566	9	61	55	49
ES-3	"Generous"	831		357	284	212	11	45	36	27
	"Spartan"	688		217	144	71	8	33	23	12
ES-4	"Generous"	699		228	155	83	8	34	24	13
	"Spartan"	590	3	119	47	−26	8	22	10	−3
ES-5	"Generous"	561		30	−43	−115	17	18	5	−8
	"Spartan"	541	54	10	−62	−135	17	15	2	−12

Notes: Rate of real growth of per capita GDP: 2% per year.

Enrollment scenarios: The five scenarios for coverage or enrollment are described on pages 16–18.

Resource mobilization scenarios: Scenarios 1–3 assume a budget allocation for education of 20%, 23%, and 26%, respectively; see also pages 43–44.

Shaded cells: Dependency on external financing 35% or less.

References

AFD (Agence Française de Développement). 2009. "Priorities for Education Finance and External Aid to Support Africa's Development in the Coming Years." PowerPoint presentation by Michel Jacquier, deputy CEO of AFD, held at the Conference of African Ministers of Finance and Education in Tunis, July 15–17.

Brossard, M., and B. Foko. 2007. *Couts et Financement de l'Enseignement Supérieur en Afrique Francophone*. Washington, DC: World Bank and Pôle de Dakar.

Bruns, B., A. Mingat, and R. Rakotomalala. 2003. *Achieving Universal Primary Education by 2015: A Chance for Every Child*. Washington, DC: World Bank.

Cohen, J., and D. Bloom. 2006. *Universal Basic and Secondary Education*. Cambridge, MA: American Academy of Arts and Sciences.

Fasih, T. 2008. *Linking Education Policy to Labor Market Outcomes*. Washington, DC: World Bank.

Fields, G. 2007. "Labor Market Policy in Developing Countries: A Selective Review of the Literature and Needs for the Future." Policy Research Working Paper 4362, World Bank, Washington, DC.

Hanushek, E., and L. Wößmann. 2007. "The Role of Education Quality in Economic Growth." Policy Research Working Paper 4122, World Bank, Washington, DC.

Hoppers, W., and S. Obeegadoo. 2008. "Beyond Primary Education: Challenges and Approaches to Expanding Learning Opportunities in Africa. Pulling the Pieces . . . Together." General Synthesis Report Presented at the ADEA 2008 Biennale on Education in Africa. Maputo, Mozambique, May 5–9.

IMF (International Monetary Fund). 2009. *World Economic Outlook April 2009: Crisis and Recovery*. World Economic and Financial Surveys. Washington, DC: IMF.

Kingdon, G., and M. Soderbom. 2008. "Education, Skills, and Labor Market Outcomes: Evidence from Ghana." Education Working Paper Series 12, World Bank, Washington, DC.

Lam, D. 2007. "The Demography of Youth in Developing Countries and Its Economic Implications." Background paper for *World Development Report 2007: Development and the Next Generation*. Washington, DC: World Bank.

Lewin, K. 2008. "Strategies for Sustainable Financing of Secondary Education in Sub-Saharan Africa." Prepared under the Secondary Education in Africa

Initiative. Working Paper 136, Africa Human Development Series, World Bank, Washington, DC.

Mingat, A. 2004. *La Rémunération/Le Statut des Enseignants dans la Perspective de l'Atteinte des Objectifs du Millénaire dans les Pàys d'Afrique Subsaharienne Francophone en 2015.* Washington, DC: World Bank.

Mingat, A., and F. Ndem. 2008. *L'Enjeu de la Scolarisation en Milieu Rural et les Défis de Développement de la Couverture Scolaire au Niveau du Premier Cycle Secondaire.* Paris: Agence Française de Développement.

UN (United Nations). 2009. *The Millennium Development Goals Report 2009.* New York: UN.

Walther, R. 2005. *Financing Vocational Training: A Europe-Africa Comparison.* Paris: Agence Française de Développement.

———. 2006. "Vocational Training in the Informal Sector." Working Paper 30, Agence Française de Développement, Paris.

Walther, R., and Filipiak, E. 2008. *Towards a Renewal of Apprenticeship in Africa.* Paris: Agence Française de Développement.

World Bank. 2008. *Accelerating Catch-Up: Tertiary Education for Growth in Sub-Saharan Africa,* Washington, DC: World Bank.

———. Forthcoming. *Education in Sub-Saharan Africa: A Comparative Analysis.* Washington, DC: World Bank.

Index

Figures, notes, and tables are indicated by *f*, *n*, and *t* following page numbers.

ECO-AUDIT
Environmental Benefits Statement

The World Bank is committed to preserving endangered forests and natural resources. The Office of the Publisher has chosen to print **Developing Post-Primary Education in Sub-Saharan Africa** on recycled paper with 30 percent post-consumer waste, in accordance with the recommended standards for paper usage set by the Green Press Initiative, a nonprofit program supporting publishers in using fiber that is not sourced from endangered forests. For more information, visit www.greenpressinitiative.org.

Saved:
- 8 trees
- 3 million BTUs of total energy
- 775 lbs of CO_2 equivalent of greenhouse gases
- 3,732 gallons of waste water
- 227 lbs of solid waste

green
press
INITIATIVE